LEARNING TO WALK BY GRACE

A Study of Romans 6-11

BIBLE STUDY GUIDE

From the Bible-teaching ministry of

Charles R. Swindoll

INSIGHT FOR LIVING

Chuck graduated in 1963 from Dallas Theological Seminary, where he now serves as the school's fourth president, helping to prepare a new generation of men and women for the ministry. Chuck has served in pastorates in three states: Massachusetts, Texas, and California, including almost twenty-three years at the First Evangelical Free Church in Fullerton, California. His sermon messages have been aired over radio since 1979 as the *Insight for Living* broadcast. A best-selling author, Chuck has written numerous books and booklets on many subjects.

Based on the outlines and transcripts of Chuck's sermons, the study guide text is co-authored by Gary Matlack, a graduate of Texas Tech University and Dallas Theological Seminary, and by Jason Shepherd, a graduate of the Texas A&M University and Dallas Theological Seminary. They also wrote the Living Insights.

Editor in Chief:	**Text Designer:**
Cynthia Swindoll	Gary Lett
Director, Educational Ministries:	**Graphic System Administrator:**
Gary Matlack	Bob Haskins
Senior Writer:	**Publishing System Specialist:**
Jason Shepherd	Alex Pasieka
Senior Editor and Assistant Writer:	**Director, Communications Division:**
Wendy Peterson	John Norton
Copy Editors:	**Project Coordinator:**
Marco Salazar	Shannon Scharkey
Glenda Schlahta	

Unless otherwise identified, all Scripture references are from the New American Standard Bible, updated edition, copyright © The Lockman Foundation 1960, 1962, 1963, 1968, 1971, 1972, 1973, 1975, 1977, 1995. Used by permission. Scripture taken from the Holy Bible, New International Version © 1973, 1978, 1984 International Bible Society, used by permission of Zondervan Bible Publishers [NIV].

Guide coauthored by Gary Matlack and Jason Shepherd:
   Copyright © 1999 by Charles R. Swindoll, Inc.
Guide edited by Bill Watkins:
   Copyright © 1985 by Charles R. Swindoll, Inc.
Outlines titled *Romans* published by New Standard for Living:
   Copyright © 1978 by Charles R. Swindoll, Inc.
Original outlines, charts, and transcripts:
   Copyright © 1976 by Charles R. Swindoll, Inc.

An effort has been made to locate sources and obtain permission where necessary for the quotations used in this book. In the event of any unintentional omission, a modification will gladly be incorporated in future printings.

ISBN 1-57972-187-7

Study Guide Cover Design: Eric Chimenti

Cover Photograph: PhotoDisc

Printed in the United States of America

CONTENTS

Key Words and Concepts in Romans   xv

Romans chart   xxii

1   Dying to Live   1
    Romans 6:1–14

2   Whose Slave Are You?   9
    Romans 6:15–23

3   Portrait of a Struggling Christian   15
    Romans 7

4   Talking about Walking   24
    Romans 8:1–13

5   A Spirit-Controlled Mind-Set   33
    Romans 8:12–17

6   The Glory and the Groan   40
    Romans 8:16–27

7   Providence Made Practical   50
    Romans 8:28–30

8   We Overwhelmingly Conquer   59
    Romans 8:31–39

9   God, the Jew, and You Too   68
    Romans 9–11

10 Straight Talk about Predestination   75
    Romans 9

11 Straight Talk about Responsibility   84
    Romans 10

12 The Jew: Cast Off or Set Aside?   91
    Romans 11:1–14

13 Horticultural Ethics   98
    Romans 11:15–29

14 Unsearchable, Unfathomable, Unmatched   105
    Romans 11:30–36

Books for Probing Further   113

Notes   117

Ordering Information   121

NOTE TO THE READER

If you're using this study guide with the broadcasts or tapes, you'll notice there's not a one-to-one correspondence between the chapters and the audio material. There are sixteen broadcast messages and only fourteen study guide chapters. Two of Chuck's messages—"Free Spirit" (Rom. 7:24–8:4) and "Providence Made Personal" (Selected Scriptures)—seemed better suited to stand on their own as broadcast messages, so their content has been blended into two other study guide chapters. The "Free Spirit" message has been absorbed into chapter 3, "Portrait of a Struggling Christian." And you'll find the heart of "Providence Made Personal" in chapter 7, "Providence Made Practical." We hope this note will prevent any confusion. May you be blessed as you study.

INTRODUCTION

You probably won't find a more significant section of New Testament Scripture than Romans 6–11.

Are there more encouraging words than Paul's message in Romans 6 of our freedom in Christ? What could be more honest and open about the Christian's struggle in this life than Romans 7? Romans 8 comforts us with life in the Spirit and God's unfailing love for His children. And Romans 9, 10, and 11 stretch our thinking and challenge our preconceptions about God's sovereignty, human responsibility, and Israel's destiny.

As you work your way through this central core of Paul's letter to the Romans, keep in mind that this is not bedside reading for the casual Christian. You will need to concentrate as you follow the logic of theological thought. But for those who are diligent in pursuing truth, God will open wide the doors of understanding.

So as you begin, pray for the Spirit to illumine your mind, to help you think God's thoughts after Him. And through God's grace in Christ, may your walk with the Savior be strengthened by time spent in His Word.

Chuck Swindoll

PUTTING TRUTH INTO ACTION

Knowledge apart from application falls short of God's desire for His children. He wants us to apply what we learn so that we will change and grow. This study guide was prepared with these goals in mind. As you go through the following pages, we hope your desire to discover biblical truth will grow as your understanding of God's Word increases and that you will be encouraged to apply what you've learned.

To assist you in your study, we've included a section called Living Insights at the end of each lesson. These exercises will challenge you to study further and to think of specific ways to put your discoveries into action.

There are many ways to use this guide—in personal devotions, group studies, discussions with friends and family, and Sunday school classes. And, of course, it's an ideal study aid when you're listening to its corresponding *Insight for Living* radio series.

To benefit most from this study guide, we would encourage you to consider it a spiritual journal. That's why we've included space in the Living Insights for recording your thoughts and discoveries. We hope you'll return to those sections often for review and encouragement as you continue to grow in your walk with Christ.

Gary Matlack
Coauthor of Text
Coauthor of Living Insights

Jason Shepherd
Coauthor of Text
Coauthor of Living Insights

LEARNING TO WALK BY GRACE

A Study of Romans 6-11

KEY WORDS AND CONCEPTS IN ROMANS

We offer this list of theological terms to help you more fully understand and apply the rich truths found in Paul's letter to the Romans. We suggest you read through the list as you begin your study, then use it as a reference guide while working your way through Romans.

Condemnation: God's judicial pronouncement of sinful humanity's guilt before Him. It is a declaration of our depravity and the punishment we deserve for it. Condemnation is the opposite of justification, which is God's pronouncement of our righteousness in Christ. Once we place our trust in Christ, we are no longer under condemnation (Rom. 8:1). Rather, we are justified—pronounced righteous by God because we are clothed in the righteousness of His Son (Rom. 3:21–26; 5:1–2, 9).

Faith: The unqualified acceptance of and dependence on the completed work of Jesus Christ to secure God's mercy toward believers. It is the instrumental cause of our salvation, the means by which we are linked to Christ and allowed to receive God's gracious gift of justification. True faith includes *knowledge* that there is a holy God who gave His Son to reconcile sinners to Himself; *assent*, which means being intellectually convinced of the truth of that knowledge; and *volition*, being so convinced of the truth that we place our trust in Christ (Rom. 1:17; 3:22, 30; Heb. 11:1).

Flesh: Used in a theological sense, *flesh* doesn't refer to our physical body. Rather, it refers to our orientation and identity before God saved us—we were unbelievers, controlled and enslaved by sin, rejecters of God, people who preferred sin over righteousness. The flesh still tries to control us, but it no longer has any claim on us, since as Christians we now belong to Christ and walk in His Spirit (see Rom. 7:5, 14, 18, 25; 8:9).

Foreknowledge: In its most general sense, *foreknowledge* is God's knowing all things before they come to pass. It is more, though, than God's simply having information ahead of time. God knows what will come to pass because He determines what will come to pass (see *predestination*). When specifically applied to salvation, foreknowledge is God's knowing us before we knew Him, before He even created us. When the Bible speaks of God's knowing people, it means He has made them the objects of His special love. Foreknowledge, then, is a word of determined choosing. God loved believers and chose them to be His own long before they put their trust in Him. To say that God foreknew us is to say He "foreloved" us (Acts 2:23; Rom. 8:29; 1 Pet. 1:1–2).

Glorification: The consummation of salvation. It occurs, in one sense, when we die and enter the presence of the Lord. At that point we will be completely free from the presence of sin. Glorification, however, occurs at its fullest when all who have died in Christ—as well as believers who are alive at Christ's return—will receive perfect, incorruptible bodies that will last for eternity. The process of sanctification will then be complete. We will be with Jesus and like Jesus—free from the presence of sin and perfect in body and soul (Rom. 8:23, 30; 1 Cor. 15:50–54; 1 John 3:2).

Gospel: The gospel, in a phrase, is "the joyous proclamation of God's redemptive activity in Christ Jesus on behalf of man enslaved by sin."[1] When we embrace the gospel by faith, we believe that Jesus lived and died for us, paying the penalty for our sins and providing us forgiveness; and that He was raised victoriously and bodily from the grave and lives for us today. All of this is motivated and accomplished by God's grace. This good news of salvation in Christ appears in the Old Testament in the form of promises, prophecies, and foreshadowing images (e.g., the promise of a redeemer in Genesis 3:15, the Passover lamb in Exodus 12, the prophecy of Christ's crucifixion in Isaiah 53, and the sacrificial system detailed in Leviticus). In the New Testament, the bright truth of the gospel bursts forth in all its glory. The four Gospels present the words and works of Christ. Acts chronicles the spread of the gospel in the known world, and the epistles explain the gospel and all its implications for

---

1. Robert H. Mounce, "Gospel," in *Evangelical Dictionary of Theology,* ed. Walter A. Elwell (Grand Rapids, Mich.: Baker Books, 1984), p. 472.

living the Christian life. And Revelation promises the consummation of our salvation, as Christ returns to claim His church. Not surprisingly, Paul used the word *gospel* some sixty times in his epistles. The message of salvation in Christ and all that means for living was the core of his message and mission (Rom. 1:15–17; 1 Cor. 15:1–4; Gal. 1:6–9; Phil. 1:12).

Grace: Unmerited favor freely granted to believers in Christ. When we say we're saved by grace, we mean that salvation comes to us, not by our ability to earn God's favor or live up to His standards, but by His free gift to us. Although salvation is a free gift, it cost God a great deal—the incarnation and death of His Son. One writer defined grace with the acrostic God's Riches At Christ's Expense.[2] Instead of receiving the judgment we deserve for our sin, we will spend an eternity in the blessed presence of our Lord. All because of grace (Rom. 5:15–17, 21; 6:14; Eph. 2:4–8; Titus 3:4–7).

Justification: God's declaration or pronouncement that sinners, upon believing in Christ, are righteous because of Christ—even though still in a sinning state (Rom. 3:23–24; Gal. 3:11). As such, we are assured of God's blessings toward us and need no longer fear His wrath or condemnation. Justification is an instantaneous act of God that begins the Christian life. Once justified (declared righteous), the Christian begins the process of sanctification (growing in Christ).

Law: God's moral demands on His created human beings. The Law reflects God's holy character and His purposes for the people He created. His Law is summarized in the Ten Commandments (Exod. 20:1–17) and more fully explained by Jesus in the Gospels (Matt. 5:21–22, 27–28) and by Paul and other New Testament writers. God's Law in the Old Testament included civil laws for the theocratic nation of Israel and ceremonial laws (sacrifices, kosher diet, etc.) that taught the need for moral purity. God still demands moral perfection from His human creatures. But unregenerate sinners cannot keep God's Law. They hate it, in fact. The Law exposes our sinfulness and our need for God's grace (Rom. 7:7). And that is the Law's main

---

2. As quoted by Ray C. Stedman in *Birth of the Body* (Santa Ana, Calif.: Vision House Publishers, 1974), p. 98.

purpose. It cannot make us righteous, but it drives us to Christ, who kept the Law perfectly and who clothes us with His own righteousness (Gal. 3:23–29). Once saved, Christians no longer hate the Law. They agree with God that His moral demands are good, and they strive to obey Him—not to earn salvation, but out of gratitude for salvation (Ps. 19:7–11; 119:35; Rom. 8:3–4; 12:1).

Predestination: In its wider sense, the word refers to God's predetermining whatever comes to pass—His working "all things after the counsel of His will" (Eph. 1:11b). In its narrower sense, which specifically relates to salvation, predestination refers to God's selecting out of sinful humanity a multitude of people He would save through Christ (Rom. 8:29; Eph. 1:4–6; see also Jer. 1:5). This narrower sense of predestination is also referred to as election. Election is closely related to foreknowledge but differs from it in that foreknowledge tells us God loved us in eternity past, whereas election tells us what that love accomplished—our salvation.

Propitiation: The satisfaction of God's wrath against sin through the sacrifice of His Son on the cross (Rom. 3:25–26). God is holy; humanity is sinful. Because God cannot excuse or condone sin, He must punish it. In His grace, He sent Jesus Christ to suffer His wrath in our place. Thus, the Cross upholds God's character as both a righteous Judge and a merciful Savior—the just One and the One who justifies (Rom. 3:26).

Righteousness: When applied to God, the word refers to His good, perfect, and holy nature and His ability to do only what is right. God cannot sin. He cannot condone sin. He cannot be unjust. And He cannot err. He always and in every way acts in accord with His perfect moral nature. When applied to humans, righteousness is what God demands of us in terms of how we live. He requires that we live in perfect obedience to His moral law— that we conform to it inwardly as well as outwardly. Since no one is able to do this (Paul says in Romans 3:10 that "there is none righteous, not even one"), someone must earn righteousness for us. That's what Jesus did. He lived a perfectly obedient life under the Law. His every thought, motive, action, and word was pleasing to the Father. Then He died on the cross to take the punishment for our *unrighteousness*. When we put our trust in Jesus, His righteousness is imputed to us—that is, God counts us as righteous, even though we still sin . . . because Christ has given His righteousness to us. Believers grow in righteousness in this life but will never be perfectly righteous until heaven.

Salvation: God's delivering us from the penalty, power, and presence of sin. Immediately upon believing in Jesus, we are delivered from the penalty of sin (eternal damnation) and the power of sin (its mastery over our lives). When we finally see the Lord face-to-face, we will be free from the presence of sin. Salvation includes not only our souls but our bodies as well, which will be resurrected on the last day.

Sanctification: When we put our trust in Christ, we were made righteous *positionally*; God declared us righteous (justified us) because of the life and death of His Son. But justification also marks the beginning of sanctification—the process of our becoming righteous *practically*, being set apart to God by the Spirit to grow out of sin and more fully into Christ. We will never be perfectly sanctified until heaven, but we will move toward perfection. We will change. We will, by the power of the Holy Spirit, conform more and more to the will of God and live lives that are pleasing to Him (Rom. 6:19; 1 Thess. 4:3–7; 5:23). Sin will always be present with us in this life, but its influence over us will be lessened over time in the process of sanctification.

Sin: Sin is both a condition and an expression. We are sinful by nature, born corrupt (Ps. 51:5; Rom. 3:10–11; Eph. 2:1). And that condition naturally produces thoughts and actions that violate God's Law (Gal. 5:19–21). Salvation in Christ is the only way to escape God's wrath toward sin and enter a life in which sin no longer controls us. Christians have the assurance that we will be free once and for all from the presence of sin when we step out of this life and into the next.

Works: We can view human works in two ways. One is to see them as deeds performed to earn God's favor so that He will repay us with salvation. The Bible is very clear that such a system of salvation is futile, since none of us can live righteously enough to keep God's Law (Rom. 3:9–18, 20; Gal. 3:10). That is why we must trust in Christ, whose works were perfect under the Law (Rom. 3:21–26; 5:6–11; 2 Cor. 5:21; Heb. 4:15). The Christian, however, has a second way to view works: good works grow out of our new life in Christ (Rom. 6:1–2, 11–13; 8:29; Gal. 5:22–24; Eph. 2:8–10; James 2:14–26; 1 John 3:16–19; 4:19–21). Indwelled by God's Spirit and in gratitude for what Christ has done for us, Christians do deeds that are pleasing to Him. When we sin, however, we need to remember that our salvation is still secure and that we have forgiveness, thanks to the perfect lawkeeping and sacrificial death of Jesus.

ROMANS

THE GOSPEL...

Introduction—Personal (1:1–17)

Conclusion—Relational (15:14–16:27)

	... Saving the Sinner	... Concerning Israel	... Concerning Christian Conduct
	Depravity of humanity	Divine sovereignty and human will	Social
	Grace of God	Past, present, and future of the nation	Civil
	Justification by faith		Personal
	Sanctification through the Spirit		
	Security of the saint		
	CHAPTERS 1:18–8:39	*CHAPTERS 9–11*	*CHAPTERS 12:1–15:13*
Emphasis	Doctrinal	National	Practical
Response	Faith	Hope	Love
Doctrine of God	Wrath	Righteousness	Glory	Grace
Doctrine of Humanity	Fallen	Dead	Saved	Struggling	Freed
Doctrine of Sin	Exposed	Conquered	Explained	Forgiven
Scope	Dead in sin	Dead to sin	Peace with God	Love for others
Main Theme	God's righteousness is given to those who put their faith in Jesus Christ.		
Key Verses	1:16–17		

Chapter 1

DYING TO LIVE

Romans 6:1–14

The sixth chapter of Romans marks a new stage in Paul's argument for the gospel. Commentator John Stott does an excellent job of reviewing where we've been (Rom. 1–5) and letting us know where we're going.

> The apostle has been painting an idyllic picture of the people of God. Having been justified by faith, they are standing in grace and rejoicing in glory. Having formerly belonged to Adam, the author of sin and death, they now belong to Christ, the author of salvation and life. Although at one point in the history of Israel the law was added to increase sin (5:20a), yet "grace increased all the more" (5:20b), so that "grace might reign" (5:21). It is a splendid vision of the triumph of grace. Against the grim background of human guilt, Paul depicts grace increasing and grace reigning.
>
> But is his picture not unbalanced? In his concentration on the secure status of the people of God, he has said little or nothing about Christian life or growth or discipleship. He seems to have jumped straight from justification to glorification, without any intervening stage of sanctification. By this omission (so far) he has exposed himself to misrepresentation by his critics. Already they have "slanderously" misquoted him as saying, "Let us do evil that good may result" (3:8). At that point he dismissed their charge, but he did not answer it. Now, however, as

1

they rally to the attack, he refutes their slander. This is the topic of Romans 6.[1]

Let's join Paul to see how we're to live the Christian life in light of God's inexhaustible grace.

The Facts of Our Position

Paul had explained at the end of chapter 5 that "the Law came in so that transgression would increase" (v. 20a). That is, so that we would see how vastly sinful we are in light of the holiness of God's standard. "But," Paul continued, "where sin increased, grace abounded all the more" (v. 20b). Where our sins are so many and so extensive, God's grace is vaster still. What a reason for the Christian to celebrate! Paul's critics, however, distorted the beauty of God's grace and accused Paul of teaching that unlimited grace encourages sin! To this Paul answers that God's grace frees us *from* sin—not *to* sin.

> What shall we say then? Are we to continue in sin so that grace may increase? May it never be! (Rom. 6:1–2a)

Using grace as permission to sin is unthinkable to Paul. Is that the way to live in light of God's kindness—sin all the more so that He has more opportunities to display His mercy? "May it never be!" exclaims Paul. "God forbid," the old King James says. We might say, "No way!" "Absolutely not!" "Impossible!" or "Ridiculous!" As commentator John A. Witmer makes clear, "In no way is the abundance of God's grace designed to encourage sin."[2]

Dead to Sin

Why does Paul so strongly reject this idea? Because we have died to sin.

> How shall we who died to sin still live in it? Or do you not know that all of us who have been baptized

---

1. John Stott, *Romans: God's Good News for the World* (Downers Grove, Ill.: InterVarsity Press, 1994), p. 166.

2. John A. Witmer, "Romans," in *The Bible Knowledge Commentary*, New Testament edition, ed. John F. Walvoord and Roy B. Zuck (Colorado Springs, Colo.: Chariot Victor Publishing, 1983), p. 461.

into Christ Jesus have been baptized into His death?
(vv. 2b–3)

What exactly is Paul saying? In order to understand his meaning, it will be helpful to see these verses in the light of verse 10:

> For the death that [Christ] died, He died to sin once for all; but the life that He lives, He lives to God.

When Christ died on the cross, He acted as our substitute and paid the penalty for sin on our behalf—the guilt of our sins can no longer condemn us. "Having died," James Montgomery Boice explains, "that phase of his life is past and will never be repeated."[3] Since we, as believers in Christ, are now reconciled and united with Him, we also have died to sin. "That old life of sin in Adam is past for us. . . . We have been brought from that old life, the end of which was death, into a new life, the end of which is righteousness."[4]

Obviously, this doesn't mean that our struggle with sin is over. Paul elsewhere presents our battle with it as a normal part of the Christian life (see Rom. 6:12–13; 13:12–14; Gal. 5:13, 16–17; 6:1; Eph. 4:25–32; Col. 3:8–10). Rather, Paul's point is that we are no longer under sin's reign, its mastery. We have crossed over from death into life, through the life-giving death of Jesus Christ. Which, as Paul illustrates, is what our baptism depicts.

> Those who believe in Christ are *baptized into* him and *baptized into* his death; in other words, they are united with him. As he died, we die to our old, sinful life-style, and a *new life* begins. Immersion may have been the form of baptism—that is, new Christians were completely buried momentarily in water. They understood this form of baptism to symbolize being buried with Christ, thus the death and burial of the old way of life. Coming up out of the water symbolized resurrection to new life with Christ, as well as the promise of a future bodily resurrection.[5]

---

3. James Montgomery Boice, *Romans, Volume 2: The Reign of Grace (Romans 5:1–8:39)* (Grand Rapids, Mich.: Baker Book House, 1992), p. 654.

4. Boice, *Romans, Volume 2*, p. 655.

5. Bruce B. Barton, David R. Veerman, and Neil Wilson, *Romans*, Life Application Bible Commentary Series (Wheaton, Ill.: Tyndale House Publishers, 1992), p. 115.

Alive in Christ

Paul next turns to the new life we share with Christ.

> Therefore we have been buried with Him through
> baptism into death, so that as Christ was raised from
> the dead through the glory of the Father, so we too
> might walk in newness of life. For if we have become
> united with Him in the likeness of His death, cer-
> tainly we shall also be in the likeness of His resur-
> rection. (Rom. 6:4–5)

Paul isn't just talking about our eventual bodily resurrection
that will take place during the end times, although that idea is
undoubtedly included. What he is talking about here is living the
resurrected life now, on earth. A life free from sin's domination, a
life of "newness." The Greek word for *newness, kainotēs,* "speaks of
life that has a new or fresh quality. The resurrection of Jesus was
not just a resuscitation; it was a new form of life."[6]

So we are dead to sin and alive in Christ. These are facts for
all who have put their trust in Him—facts as real as His historical
death and resurrection. Paul, though, is doing more than dispensing
information here. He's giving us words of life.

Living Out Our Position

In verses 6–14, Paul sets forth a three-part plan for living out
our new life. First, we're to *know* that our old self was crucified with
Christ and that we're alive in Him (vv. 6, 8). Second, we're to
consider ourselves dead to sin (v. 11). And third, we're to *present*
ourselves to God as those alive in Christ (v. 13). *Know, consider,
present*—three words that tell us much about walking in the new
life our Savior has won for us.

What We Need to Know

> *Knowing* this, that our old self was crucified with
> Him, in order that our body of sin might be done
> away with, so that we would no longer be slaves to
> sin; for he who has died is freed from sin.
>
> Now if we have died with Christ, we believe
> that we shall also live with Him, *knowing* that Christ,

6. Witmer, "Romans," p. 462.

having been raised from the dead, is never to die again; death no longer is master over Him. For the death that He died, He died to sin once for all; but the life that He lives, He lives to God. (vv. 6–10, emphasis added)

Right living grows out of right thinking. So walking with Christ begins with knowing how His death and resurrection affect us. Paul says that our "old self" was crucified with Christ. What exactly is the "old self"?

The believer before he or she trusted Christ, the person who was ruled by sin and was God's enemy (5:10). Some think that Paul distinguishes between two parts or two natures in man; so it is debated whether the new nature replaces the old nature or whether the new nature is added to the old. But the "old man" and the "new man" are not parts of our personality; rather, they describe our orientation to the old life in Adam or the new life in Christ.[7]

And living the new life in Christ begins with knowing. Knowing that He died to set us free from sin. Knowing that our old self was nailed to the cross with Him. Knowing that, just as Jesus rose from the dead and will live forever, we have been raised to a new life in Him that has no end. A life no longer ruled by the tyranny of sin. But there's more.

What We Need to Consider

Even so consider yourselves to be dead to sin, but alive to God in Christ Jesus. (Rom. 6:11)

The word *consider*

conveys the idea of reckoning or calculating. Perhaps here "regard" or "recognize" would help us understand that Paul is arguing that his readers should come to see the truth of their situation. Christ's death and resurrection has altered their position, and they should live in accordance with the new reality. . . . This does not mean that he is immune to sinning.

7. Barton, Veerman, and Wilson, *Romans*, p. 117.

Paul does not say that sin is dead but that the believer is to count himself as dead to it. He feels temptation and sometimes he sins. But the sin of the unbeliever is the natural consequence of the fact that he is a slave to sin, whereas the sin of the believer is quite out of character. He has been set free.[8]

We have not, however, only been freed *from* something. We've also been freed *for* something. We're free to love and serve God. Therefore, we're to reckon ourselves "alive to God in Christ Jesus."

This should come as a relief to many who limit the Christian life to simply doing the right things. It's true that this life is intended to be observable and ethical, not obscure and ethereal. Jesus, after all, said, "If you love Me, you will keep My commandments" (John 14:15). And James wrote, "But prove yourselves doers of the word, and not merely hearers who delude themselves" (James 1:22). But it is on the basis of the life, death, and resurrection of Jesus that we can even move in the direction of living for God. And when we fail to live as God commands, we can rest assured that the righteousness of Christ covers all our sins and that forgiveness is there for the asking (see 1 John 1:9).

Knowing the truth, then, and recognizing (considering) its application to our lives—these logically lead to the next step: presenting ourselves to God.

What We Need to Present

Therefore do not let sin reign in your mortal body so that you obey its lusts, and do not go on presenting the members of your body to sin as instruments of unrighteousness; but present yourselves to God as those alive from the dead, and your members as instruments of righteousness to God. For sin shall not be master over you, for you are not under law but under grace. (Rom. 6:12–14)

We can live for God because we've been set free from sin. Righteous living is rooted in redemption. That's why it's futile for anyone to try to live a "good life" without Christ.

---

8. Leon Morris, *The Epistle to the Romans* (1988; reprint, Grand Rapids, Mich.: William B. Eerdmans Publishing Co., 1992), p. 256.

Notice that Paul's instruction includes both negative and positive aspects—the avoidance of sin and the pursuit of righteousness. The Christian life can't be reduced to staying away from the bad stuff. A growing Christian will also long to love and serve God, to pursue the things that honor and glorify Him.

So, even though we will never be able to completely turn our backs on sin in this life or be completely free from our struggle with it, we are no longer under its dominion. Sin doesn't own us, even though it still tries. Christ owns us. He is our Master. And He has won the victory over sin and death for us. One day, in heaven, we will step into the fullness of that victory. For now, though, the battle rages. So we trust in the truth of our deliverance.

 Living Insights

Romans 6:1–14 supplies a crucial principle: Correct theology must precede right living. Ethics without theology means frustration for those wanting to live a life unto God. If we reduce the Christian life to just doing our best or merely following Jesus' moral example, we miss the whole basis for it. Living right grows out of our union with Christ. His death to sin is our death to sin. His resurrection is our resurrection to new life. That is where the power and confidence to live for Christ come from.

Sometimes, though, our personal struggle with particular sins can obscure the fact that we are in union with Christ. We adopt an attitude that says, "Well, Christ died to save me, but I guess it's up to me to live right from here on out." Paul would tell us during such times, "Know . . . consider . . . present." *Know* that who you once were has been crucified with Christ and that you are a new creation, raised to new life. *Consider*, recognize, remind yourself that you are dead to sin and alive to Christ. And *present* this new life to God for His glory and service.

Sin will always be with us this side of heaven. But so will the truth of Christ's saving us from it. And that truth, as Jesus promised, will set us free:

> So Jesus was saying to those Jews who had believed Him, "If you continue in My word, then you are truly disciples of Mine; and you will know the truth, and the truth will make you free." (John 8:31–32)

Is there a part of your life that makes you wonder if you're living as you should be? An ongoing struggle with a particular sin? Nagging doubts? Personal conflict? Write your concerns down.

_____

_____

_____

How can the truth of this lesson help you in your struggle? Has it encouraged you that you're not on your own? That Christ's death and resurrection are as important for living out your faith (sanctification) as they are for being saved (justification)? What have you learned?

_____

_____

_____

_____

_____

Good. Now, just remember that He has sufficient grace for whatever you face (Rom. 5:20–21; 2 Cor. 12:9).

Chapter 2
WHOSE SLAVE ARE YOU?
Romans 6:15–23

Let's step out of Romans for a moment and travel back to the days of Israel's conquest of the Promised Land. Joshua, after publicly reviewing the history of Israel's deliverance, says to the tribes assembled at Shechem:

> "Now, therefore, fear the Lord and serve Him in
> sincerity and truth; and put away the gods which
> your fathers served beyond the River and in Egypt,
> and serve the Lord. If it is disagreeable in your sight
> to serve the Lord, choose for yourselves today whom
> you will serve: whether the gods which your fathers
> served which were beyond the River, or the gods of
> the Amorites in whose land you are living; but as
> for me and my house, we will serve the Lord."
> (Josh. 24:14–15)

Joshua had discovered the same thing Paul would write about centuries later: You've got to serve somebody. No one is completely free—not in the sense of being absolutely independent from authority or control. We'll either love and serve the true God . . . or we'll serve whatever gods we make for ourselves—false images, ambition, desires, money, or even ourselves.

Ironically, it's only by being a slave to Christ that we are truly free. For His way leads to love, righteousness, and eternal life. Any other way leads to condemnation under the Law, the bondage of sin, and death. Why, then, would we want to be enslaved to anything or anyone but Him?

That's the question Paul explores in the last half of Romans 6.

Slavery: Different Metaphor, Same Truth

Paul begins this passage in basically the same way that he began the last.

> What then? Shall we sin because we are not under
> law but under grace? May it never be! (Rom. 6:15;
> see also v. 1)

9

In 6:1–14 Paul described our new life in Christ in terms of dying and being raised with Him. But here in verses 15–23, he communicates the same truth—the absurdity of using grace as a license to sin—with a different metaphor, that of slavery.

Slaves of Sin or Righteousness?

> Do you not know that when you present yourselves
> to someone as slaves for obedience, you are slaves of
> the one whom you obey, either of sin resulting in death,
> or of obedience resulting in righteousness? (6:16)

According to Paul, we only have two choices. We can either serve sin, which leads to death, or we can serve Christ in obedience, which leads to eternal life. The words of Jesus echo in the background of Paul's instruction:

> "No one can serve two masters; for either he will
> hate the one and love the other, or he will be de-
> voted to one and despise the other. You cannot serve
> God and wealth." (Matt. 6:24)

Jesus wasn't saying that money was evil. He was saying that we can't be equally devoted to God and our own appetite for material things. Paul presents this same exclusivity. We serve either Christ or something (or someone) else.

We're Already Slaves of Righteousness

As Christians, though, our choice of masters has already been made.

> But thanks be to God that though you were slaves
> of sin, you became obedient from the heart to that
> form of teaching to which you were committed, and
> having been freed from sin, you became slaves of
> righteousness. (Rom. 6:17–18)

What great news! The question of our ownership, our allegiance, has already been settled. "Thanks be to God" that we know who our Master is. We have heard the gospel ("that form of teaching") and trusted Jesus Christ with our hearts, our souls, our eternal destiny. That doesn't mean we'll never sin again in this life. But it does mean that Christ has rescued us from the cruel reign and mastery of sin and brought us under His benevolent ownership.

Notice how often in Romans 6 Paul reminds his readers of their position in Christ—that which is *already* true of them. They have died to sin (6:2). They have been baptized into Christ's death and resurrection (vv. 3–5). Their old selves were crucified with Him (v. 6). They are free from sin (v. 7). They now live for God (vv. 8–11). They are not under law but under grace (v. 14).

Living the Christian life to its fullest begins with knowing what Christ has done for us, not what we must do for Him. We have what we need to live the Christian life: the positional truth of His having lived, died, and risen for us; our having died and risen with Him; our new life of freedom from sin—all of these and more. Before we can do for Christ, we must know what He has done for us. No wonder, in reflecting on our Savior's goodness to us, Paul breaks out in thanks (v. 17)!

An Ongoing and Increasing Slavery

Paul inserts an apology in verse 19 for speaking to his readers in "human terms," meaning his use of the slavery metaphor. This has been necessary, however, due to the "weakness of [their] flesh." Perhaps sin or apathy or some other condition has caused many of his readers to fail to consider their new life in Christ. So, to make his point, Paul has chosen to describe that new life in terms they can grasp.

His disclaimer for this imagery is understandable, since the metaphor of slavery doesn't completely do justice to the new Christian's freedom in Christ. The topic of slavery in Paul's day, after all, would have conjured up images of cruelty and oppression. But the Christian's enslavement to Christ puts him or her under a light yoke, a loving Master, and a life free from the oppression of legalism (see Matt. 11:28–30). No earthly image can fully represent the love and grace Christ has lavished on His own. Nonetheless, the analogy of slavery is helpful in describing the change of allegiance and domination—from sin to Christ.

It's also helpful to understand that slavery is an ongoing condition rather than a one-time purchase.

> For just as you presented your members as slaves to impurity and to lawlessness, resulting in further lawlessness, so now present your members as slaves to righteousness, resulting in sanctification. (v. 19b)

The longer we are slaves to sin, the more enslaved to sin we become. We deteriorate morally. But once we are set free from sin and set apart to God as slaves of righteousness, instead of deteriorating, we progress—we grow in Christlikeness. This is known as the process of sanctification. And how do we participate in it? By presenting our "members as slaves to righteousness." By continuing to pursue the thoughts, attitudes, and activities that God loves and that evidence our relationship with Christ.

The Outcome of Our Slavery: Eternal Life

Continuing with the idea of where slavery leads—either to sin or to righteousness, Paul writes:

> For when you were slaves of sin, you were free in regard to righteousness. Therefore what benefit were you deriving from the things of which you are now ashamed? For the outcome of those things is death. But now having been freed from sin and enslaved to God, you derive your benefit, resulting in sanctification, and the outcome, eternal life. (vv. 20–22)

Slavery to one thing is freedom from another. When we were enslaved to sin, for example, we were "free" in regard to righteousness. But what kind of freedom was that? It seems freeing to follow sin, but such a life leads only to degradation and death.

On the other hand, slavery to God in Jesus Christ is the only true freedom. For that life leads to sanctification and eventually to eternal life.

To further differentiate the life of sin from life in Christ, Paul draws one more analogy.

> For the wages of sin is death, but the free gift of God is eternal life in Christ Jesus our Lord. (v. 23)

Deserved payment versus an undeserved gift. That's Paul's imagery here. Death is a wage rightly paid for a life of sin. Physical death occurs because we live in a world contaminated by Adam's and Eve's original sin. And spiritual, eternal death awaits those who remain in that sin and do not turn to Christ for forgiveness. That's what we deserve. But God gives us what we don't deserve—the free gift of eternal life in Jesus Christ.

So let us live gratefully and thankfully to God for the gift He has given us. And let us live as slaves of righteousness to our benevolent Master—the only way to be truly free.

 ## *Living Insights*

What does it mean to "present your members as slaves to righteousness, resulting in sanctification" (6:19)? *Members* typically refers to various parts of the body, but Paul obviously also had in mind "every part that goes into making up [the] person."[1] This would include thoughts, choices, attitudes, philosophies, actions, habits, and so on. All of these are subject now to our new Master, Christ, and are being renewed in Him. So presenting our members as slaves of righteousness means living deliberately under the reign of Christ, seeing every part of our being as subject to His rule.

Why not take some time right now to evaluate how you're doing at presenting yourself as a slave of righteousness? Hopefully, you'll be encouraged that Christ is at work in your life and that His loving ownership of you is yielding recognizable changes.

How do you find yourself using your time lately? To pursue a closer walk with Christ? To study His Word? To build up His body? For some other purpose?

_____

_____

_____

How do you make decisions these days? By wisdom that comes from the Word of God? Through the lens of pleasing your new Master Christ or your old master sin? What philosophies, positions, beliefs are being challenged or changed because of the Spirit's work in your heart?

_____

_____

_____

1. Leon Morris, *The Epistle to the Romans* (1988; reprint, Grand Rapids, Mich.: William B. Eerdmans Publishing Co., 1992), p. 265.

What behaviors that have plagued you in the past seem to be improving because of Christ's work in your life?

_____

_____

_____

What areas of thought or behavior are still a struggle for you?

_____

_____

_____

What "members" can you present in a new way to facilitate change?

_____

_____

_____

Chapter 3

PORTRAIT OF A STRUGGLING CHRISTIAN
Romans 7

Let's face it. We don't like to struggle . . . with anything. Period. Given a choice, most of us would rather have what we want when we want it without having to work or fight for it. Material provisions without sweating for them. Great relationships minus the conflict and confrontation. Excellent health and physique apart from diet and exercise. Computer acumen with no learning curve. And, oh yes, instant spiritual maturity.

But life doesn't work that way, does it? Not the professional life. Not the relational life. Not the physical or intellectual life. And definitely not the spiritual life.

That doesn't mean everything about the spiritual life is hard work for us. Our eternal destiny, after all, has been settled—thanks to Jesus' work. Once we put our faith in Him, our salvation is secure. God has declared us righteous on account of His Son; our justification is complete.

Our *sanctification*, however, is ongoing. As we grow in our faith, sin is always there trying to lure us back. And, though sin can never again own or master us, it can certainly influence us. It can even convince us from time to time to try living for ourselves instead of for Christ.

So Christian growth doesn't come without a struggle. And Paul explores that struggle—his and ours—in Romans 7.

Romans 7 in Context

Speaking of struggles, studying Romans 7 is no cakewalk. In fact, Paul seems downright hard to follow at times. Theologians vary as to exactly what Paul is saying, especially in the last half of the chapter. So, before we dive into these rich and challenging verses, let's try to get a handle on the big picture.

This chapter contains material from Chuck's message "Free Spirit."

To begin with, let's remember where we are in the book of Romans. We're in the section where Paul is describing the process of sanctification (chaps. 6–8). Justification is an accomplished event for the Christian—a truth Paul set forth in 3:21–5:21. So, by the time we get to Romans 6, the Christian is already justified—pronounced righteous in Christ, already a believer. From there Paul shifts to a discussion of how the new believer moves forward in the Christian life.

He exposes the foolishness of continuing to offer ourselves to a life of sin when we have been set free from its mastery. We now serve a new Master—Christ. Our new life of service to Him results in righteousness, holiness, and eternal life (chap. 6). Now freed from sin and forgiven in Christ, we are released from the Law's condemning hold, as Paul illustrates in chapter 7. As believers, we now love God's Law and want to pursue it. But can we do it in our own strength? Absolutely not. That's why Paul shows us in Romans 8 that sanctification comes only through the Holy Spirit, who indwells and empowers us and conforms us to Christ's image.

To summarize, Romans 6–8 progresses like this:

Romans 6: Freed from sin
Romans 7: Freed from the Law
Romans 8: Free to live by the Spirit

Does free mean easy? No way. As long as we're living on this side of heaven, we will struggle with the flesh. In theological language, *positional* freedom in Christ doesn't guarantee constant *experiential* freedom from our sin nature. Paul's goal in chapter 7 is to relate the nature of this struggle before revealing the divine Helper God has provided us in chapter 8.

An Exposition of Romans 7

To get a handle on this sizable chunk of Scripture, it will be helpful to break it down into three smaller sections. In verses 1–6, Paul presents the Christian's freedom from the Law. In verses 7–13, he defends the goodness of the Law and upholds its true purpose: to expose sin. And in verses 14–25, he reveals the futility of trying to conquer the flesh through the Law. As diverse as these three sections sound, they actually flow together to make a powerful exhortation to trust Christ and His Spirit for living the Christian life.

16

Freedom from the Law

Just as Paul used the analogy of slavery in chapter 6, now he uses the metaphor of marriage to illustrate our freedom from the Law.

> Or do you not know, brethren (for I am speaking to those who know the law), that the law has jurisdiction over a person as long as he lives? For the married woman is bound by law to her husband while he is living; but if her husband dies, she is released from the law concerning the husband. So then, if while her husband is living she is joined to another man, she shall be called an adulteress; but if her husband dies, she is free from the law, so that she is not an adulteress though she is joined to another man. (Rom. 7:1–3)

As the death of a spouse frees the remaining person to remarry, so our dying with Christ on the cross frees us from our former "spouse," the Law, to love and live for our new Betrothed (v. 4). Death changes our obligations—both in marriage and in our relationship to the Law. This doesn't mean that the Law has no value for the Christian. It does mean, though, that we're free from its condemnation. We're also free from trying to earn God's salvation by keeping the Law. We've been joined to Another—One who kept the Law perfectly and who graciously gives us His righteousness through faith.

While we were "in the flesh" (v. 5a)—that is, unsaved—we were ruled by the drive to obey our sinful desires. The Law was not only unable to save us, but it actually provoked the sin that already resided in us. As a result, we could only produce works motivated by sin, which Paul calls bearing "fruit for death" (v. 5b).

Now, however, we have been set free from the Law. As Paul tells us,

> But now we have been released from the Law, having died to that by which we were bound, so that we serve in newness of the Spirit and not in oldness of the letter. (v. 6)

This doesn't mean that the Law is erased or that it is bad; Paul later says that it is "holy and righteous and good" (v. 12). What it does mean is that righteous living comes through the Spirit's work in us, not by our own fleshly efforts to obey the Law.

Defense and Purpose of the Law

So far in Romans, Paul hasn't had a lot of good things to say about the Law.

- Its ceremonial practices, such as circumcision, have no value in terms of making people righteous (2:25).

- It cannot justify but only condemn (3:20).

- Justification comes by faith, not through the Law (3:21, 24, 28).

- Not even Abraham, the father of the Hebrews, was justified by the Law (4:2, 13).

- It "increases" sin by revealing the magnitude of our sinfulness (5:20).

- And Jesus has had to free us from the Law's condemning hold (7:6).

After such a prolonged and passionate polemic against the Law, Paul's readers may well have asked at this point, "Is there anything good about it?" For if the Law itself is faulty in some way, there must be something lacking in the God who gave it. Anticipating this question, Paul next defends the character of the Law and explains its purpose.

> What shall we say then? Is the Law sin? May it never be! On the contrary, *I would not have come to know sin except through the Law;* for I would not have known about coveting if the Law had not said, "You shall not covet." But sin, taking opportunity through the commandment, produced in me coveting of every kind; for apart from the Law sin is dead. I was once alive apart from the Law; but when the commandment came, sin became alive and I died; and this commandment, which was to result in life, proved to result in death for me; for sin, taking an opportunity through the commandment, deceived me and through it killed me. So then, *the Law is holy, and the commandment is holy and righteous and good.*
> Therefore did that which is good become a cause of death for me? May it never be! Rather it was sin, in order that it might be shown to be sin by effecting my death through that which is good, so that *through*

the commandment sin would become utterly sinful.
(7:7–13, emphasis added)

God's Law is not the problem, explains Paul; our sin is the problem. The Law is simply doing its job—exposing the depth of our sin. Whatever the Law prohibits, we pursue. Whatever the Law commands, we neglect. That's not the Law's fault. It's our fault. Being sinners by nature, we naturally do what we aren't supposed to do and don't do what we should.

We see this every day in our lives. A sign hanging on a park bench says, "Wet paint. Do not touch." And what do we do? We touch. "No U-turns." "Keep off the grass." "Don't push this button!" Our sinful nature is actually enticed to do the exact opposite of all these good and purposeful commands. Augustine speaks of this tendency in his *Confessions*. He recounts a time when, at the age of sixteen, he stole the fruit from a pear tree . . . and he didn't even like pears. He did it simply because it was forbidden.

So the Law excites and exposes sin. And it also condemns it. It reminds us that we are under a death sentence for our failure to keep God's righteous commandments (v. 10).

Now, does this truth contradict what Paul said in verse 9: "I was once alive apart from the Law; but when the commandment came, sin became alive and I died"? Weren't we dead in our trespasses and sins before we came to faith (Eph. 2:1)? Notice that Paul has shifted to the first person in this verse—"*I* was once alive . . . *I* died." Probably, he is reflecting on his life before his conversion. As a self-righteous Pharisee, Paul certainly believed he was pleasing God with his life (see Phil. 3:4–6). He thought he was keeping the Law. But when the Law *came*, that is, when God truly revealed to him that he could not keep the Law, he was convicted by that Law and "died." That is, he realized he deserved death. The Law had done its work in Paul's life.

The Futility of Trying to Conquer Our Flesh through the Law

Having explained that the Law itself is good (Rom. 7:12) and that it is sinners who are bad (v. 13), Paul turns the discussion toward the relationship between the redeemed person's sin nature and the Law (vv. 14–25).[1] His frustration with his flesh's helplessness is palpable.

---

1. In verses 7–13, Paul dealt with the Law's purpose in the lives of preconversion sinners. Now he addresses the struggle with sin for the believer.

For we know that the Law is spiritual, but I am of flesh, sold in bondage to sin. For what I am doing, I do not understand; for I am not practicing what I would like to do, but I am doing the very thing I hate. But if I do the very thing I do not want to do, I agree with the Law, confessing that the Law is good. So now, no longer am I the one doing it, but sin which dwells in me. For I know that nothing good dwells in me, that is, in my flesh; for the willing is present in me, but the doing of the good is not. For the good that I want, I do not do, but I practice the very evil that I do not want. But if I am doing the very thing I do not want, I am no longer the one doing it, but sin which dwells in me. (vv. 14–20)

These verses have been debated by theologians for centuries. The main issue centers on the identity of Paul's *I*. Is Paul speaking of himself as an unregenerate, preconversion man? Or is he speaking of himself as redeemed, now living in a state of grace? Those who take the former position cite Paul's descriptions of being "of flesh" and "sold into bondage to sin" (v. 14) as incompatible with a saved individual. Has Paul not already stated that he and all Christians are set free from sin (6:2, 14, 17–18, 22) and were formerly "in the flesh" (7:5)? How, then, could he speak of Christians in terms of slavery and flesh? Then, those who argue that Paul *is* speaking of himself as regenerate cite his joyful concurrence with God's Law (v. 22) and his serving it (v. 25) as descriptive of someone who could only be redeemed. And still others believe that Paul is speaking of himself as one under the conviction of the Law but not yet regenerate.

Without examining the pros and cons of each argument (that's a book in itself), it seems best to take Paul's description as applying to himself as a believer. He is, after all, speaking in the present tense. And the struggle he describes—desiring to do what is right and hating the wrong that he does—hardly seems likely for a person still lost in his sins and untouched by grace.

So, if we hold this perspective, then his description of himself as "of flesh" and "sold into bondage to sin" (v. 14) reflects not his actual position in Christ, for he is saved. Rather, it reflects his very realistic view of the tendencies of the old, sinful nature that still dog his steps as he grows in Christ.

In fact, the more we grow in Christ, the more aware we become of our sin and the more we hate it and want to be rid of it. Remember the prophet Isaiah, who saw a vision of the Lord seated on His throne, surrounded by angels singing His praises? So overcome was he by the splendid holiness of God that all he could say was,

"Woe is me, for I am ruined!
Because I am a man of unclean lips,
And I live among a people of unclean lips;
For my eyes have seen the King, the Lord of hosts."
(Isa. 6:5)

Therein lies the struggle of the Christian life. We love God. We're growing in Christ. We're learning more about God's grace and character. We want to love what He loves and hate what He hates. We long for the day when we are rid of sin forever. But the sinful nature, the person we were in Adam, stills calls to us and beckons us to live in rebellion against God. Paul goes on:

I find then the principle that evil is present in me, the one who wants to do good. For I joyfully concur with the law of God in the inner man, but I see a different law in the members of my body, waging war against the law of my mind and making me a prisoner of the law of sin which is in my members. Wretched man that I am! Who will set me free from the body of this death? Thanks be to God through Jesus Christ our Lord! So then, on the one hand I myself with my mind am serving the law of God, but on the other, with my flesh the law of sin. (Rom. 7:21–25)

Notice that, for Paul, this struggle between his new nature and his old nature doesn't end in despair. It ends in joyful victory. Only through Jesus Christ can we even begin to cope with the sin that remains in us. By His grace, and not by our own vain efforts to keep the Law, we no longer stand condemned under the Law. For we have received His righteousness, the merits of His perfect obedience.

And so, as the Law of God continues to show us where we fall short, we run to Christ and bask in His grace. And we learn to please God, not by trying to keep the Law in our own power, but by trusting in God's grace and, as Romans 8 will tell us, walking in step with the Spirit. For if our justification came by God's provision alone, so must our sanctification.

21

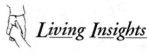

Living Insights

Once again, I proved my natural tendency to break laws instead of keep them. On a recent visit to the San Diego Wild Animal Park in California, my family and I took an hour-long tram ride through the sprawling preserve. We saw hundreds of animals roaming around in the open. Giraffes, water buffalo, antelope, wild goats, rhinos, elephants . . . it was like driving through the wilds of Africa.

As we slowed down before coming to the gorilla habitat, the tour guide cautioned us to be very quiet, because these animals spooked easily. Not that they could hurt us; they were in a secure environment. She just didn't want us to upset them. She encouraged us to get a closer look on foot later but offered this warning:

> "Never establish eye contact with an ape, and never bare your teeth. They take these as signs of aggression, and you might make them mad."

You guessed it. My first thought was, *Hey, we need to go by and see the gorillas up close, so I can test this theory.* The apes, however, were pretty lazy that day and didn't seem remotely interested in staring at the tourists who were staring at them. They were just lolling in the sun, eating; some even had their backs to us. So, no eye contact. And I actually chickened out on baring my teeth. I could just see myself getting carted off to wildlife jail for inciting a simian riot. What would my kids have thought?

The truth is, though, that part of me still gets a kind of twisted enjoyment out of breaking the rules. Now don't look so smug. You've had those thoughts too. You've even carried some of them out. We take impish delight in bucking authority and beating the system. Part of each of us still wants to break the rules—whether they are human rules or God's Law.

If we weren't Christians, we would have no hope when such thoughts arise in our minds. We would stand condemned before God. But as those who have been washed by the blood of the Lamb, we have hope. Unlike non-Christians, we have a choice. We can rejoice with Paul and say, "Thanks be to God through Jesus Christ our Lord!" (Rom. 7:25). Though sin remains in us, the Holy Spirit also indwells us so we can now love the Law of God and live a life that pleases Him (8:4). We have been freed from sin's reign. And when we blow it—when we break the Law—we can rest assured that our salvation is still secure. We are still the objects of God's love and grace. Christ's perfect law-keeping and sacrificial death cover all our sins—past, present, and future. And His mercy and grace provide us forgiveness and a fresh start (1 John 1:9).

So the next time you touch wet paint . . . or smile at an ape . . . or hate your neighbor . . . or doubt God's goodness . . . or have impure sexual thoughts, remember: The Christian life is a battle, but the war is already won. If you have placed your trust in Christ, who never broke one of God's Laws, you're on your way home. The struggle is just part of the journey.

Chapter 4

TALKING ABOUT WALKING

Romans 8:1–13

It's 3:30 P.M. in America. Thousands of boys and girls have rushed home from school, grabbed their asphalt-worn basketballs, and headed for the nearest driveway, blacktop, or gym to shoot some hoops. Some play in air-conditioned recreation centers, wearing brightly colored uniforms with logos of lions, mustangs, and Spartans. Others play pickup ball, where the uniform choices are limited to "shirts" or "skins," and the only other gear seems to be hole-ridden socks and tattered sneakers.

No matter where these young athletes play, however, all of them have one thing in common—they all want to be the next Michael Jordan. Which one of them could not sing the Gatorade jingle "I want to be like Mike"? And how many times has each one fantasized about sinking a game-winning shot with their team down by one point with the clock ticking off 3 . . . 2 . . . 1 . . . ? In their dreams, of course, they're all like Mike.

Dreams, though, seldom match reality. Statistics prove that for every boy or girl who makes it to the professional ranks, tens of thousands will live out their basketball existence playing in musty gyms and choosing their teammates by the eeny-meeny-miney-mo method. And the next Michael Jordan? Don't hold your breath—unless you also believe that someday you'll win the lottery.

In some ways, the Christian life is similar to basketball. So many of us start our spiritual journeys dreaming of being the next Paul or Ruth or David—the heroes of the Christian faith. But we learn quickly that our sinful nature accompanied us when we came to Christ. And no matter how hard we try to live like spiritual champions, our old nature seems to be right in our face at nearly every turn.

Are we, then, destined to play out our spiritual lives in the bitterness of defeat instead of in the joy of victory? Absolutely not! Though similar in some ways, Christianity and basketball are different too. We don't obtain the victory of salvation by being an all-star. Salvation doesn't come by performance; it comes by faith. And once we put our faith in Christ, our destiny is certain. We don't have to become high-profile personalities to be accepted by God. We can be a valuable player wherever He places us.

Since we're all headed for the same place, then, how can we best participate in God's plan for us to be like Christ? Let's start by taking a look at the foundational truths contained in Romans 8:1–13.

An Introduction to Romans 8

Chapter 8 has been called "the inspirational highlight of the Book of Romans."[1] The emotions in this chapter build much like a symphony—the first movement begins with God's provision of the Spirit for victory over our sin nature; the second movement swells with the sufferings that mark our present existence; and the finale crests with a doxology of praise of the unfathomable love of God revealed in Christ.

Few passages in the Bible match the power and passion expressed here by Paul. And few sections of Scripture surpass Romans 8 in revealing the awesome ministry of the Holy Spirit. Commentator Everett F. Harrison helps us see how this chapter is the culmination of so much that has preceded it.

> [Romans 8] gathers up various strands of thought from the entire discussion of both justification and sanctification and ties them together with the crowning knot of glorification. Like chapter 5, it presents the blessings of the justified life, grounded in the removal of condemnation. Like chapter 6, it stresses freedom from the bondage of sin and ultimately from the bondage of death. Like chapter 7, it deals with the problem of the flesh, finding the solution in the liberation and productive ministry of the Spirit. The chapter begins with instruction, rises to consolation, and culminates in jubilation. This is high and holy ground indeed for the Christian pilgrim to tread.[2]

Let's prepare to enter this holy ground, then, as we explore the first thirteen verses of Romans 8.

1. Robert H. Mounce, *Romans*, The New American Commentary series (Nashville, Tenn.: Broadman and Holman Publishers, 1995), vol. 27, p. 173.

2. Everett F. Harrison, "Romans," in *The Expositor's Bible Commentary*, gen. ed. Frank E. Gaebelein (Grand Rapids, Mich.: Zondervan Publishing House, Regency Reference Library, 1976), vol. 10, p. 85.

The Believer before God

In verses 1–4, three crucial and comforting truths emerge about the justified person's standing before God.

Eternally Secure

Verse 1 begins with the term *therefore,* which tells us that we need to understand the previous section in order to fully appreciate what Paul is about to say. In chapter 7, he described the battle with the sin nature, a struggle which led him to cry out, "Wretched man that I am! Who will set me free from the body of this death?" (v. 24).

We all can relate to Paul's exasperation. We've struggled against sin. We've felt the subtle yet almost irresistible riptide of temptation drawing us out to a sea of pleasure and then drowning us in its consequences. Let's read what he writes in the next verse and see what hope he offers us.

In verse 25, Paul revealed that we can be set free from the power of sin by only one thing—the atoning work of Jesus Christ. As a result, he could confidently assert that, for those in Christ, condemnation has been done away with (8:1).

> Therefore there is now no condemnation for those who are in Christ Jesus. (8:1)

Even though we will continue to struggle against our sin nature—and sometimes even lose that battle—we will never receive everlasting punishment for our failures. That's the first benefit of the atoning work of Christ—eternal security. What a wonderful reminder! How many times have we cried out like Paul, "Wretched sinner that I am!"? Although the Law would condemn us, and although we would judge and condemn ourselves, God withholds His judgment because of His grace to us in Christ and His patient love toward us.

Internally Free

The atoning work of Christ brings us a second benefit—internal freedom.

> For the law of the Spirit of life in Christ Jesus has set you free from the law of sin and death. (v. 2)

It seems like almost every salvation testimony includes a phrase similar to this one: "I felt like a heavy weight had been lifted off my shoulders." These words describe powerful and moving emotions, but what spiritual reality is at their root? Only one thing—the release from "the law of sin and death."

Like a cruel slave-owner, the law of sin and death rules every unregenerate person. It permeates everything they do, even helpful and virtuous deeds. But when they trust in Jesus Christ, the shackles fall off and believers are emancipated from their bondage. No wonder so many Christians weep when they reach this part of their testimony! What an empowering experience to finally say "No!" to the flesh and "Yes!" to the grace of God!

Every one of us, in Christ, has the ability to reject sin. We can resist temptation and choose to live righteously. This internal freedom is the second benefit of the atoning work of Christ.

Positionally Perfect

Christ's work on the cross brings another benefit—positional perfection.

> For what the Law could not do, weak as it was through the flesh, God did: sending His own Son in the likeness of sinful flesh and as an offering for sin, He condemned sin in the flesh, so that the requirement of the Law might be fulfilled in us, who do not walk according to the flesh but according to the Spirit. (vv. 3–4)

These verses tell us that, although God's Law infallibly spelled out perfect righteousness, it could not be perfectly obeyed by sinful humans. But what we could not do, God did by sending His Son. Jesus lived a perfect life, fulfilling the Law's requirements. Then He died a substitutionary death so that we could be saved.

Consequently, those of us who trust in Christ are given His righteousness. A righteousness we could not obtain on our own. A righteousness that delivers us from God's judgment. And, thanks to the indwelling Holy Spirit, we are free to love and pursue God's holy standards—a way of life that pleases Him.

Does this mean we're now perfect in every way? Obviously not. But it does mean that we are *positionally* perfect. Through Christ, our standing before God is that of someone who lived a perfect life. When the Lord looks at us, He looks at us through lenses colored by Jesus' blood. God knows that our behaviors don't always match our position, and that is why Scripture constantly encourages us to

27

"walk by the Spirit" (Gal. 5:16), to live in a manner worthy of our new station.

Living in the Flesh versus Living in the Spirit

Now that Paul has laid the foundational truths upon which we can live a victorious Christian life, he moves on to contrast that victorious life with the old life dominated by the flesh.[3]

Life according to the Flesh

In much the same way that the Hebrews in Moses' day needed to be reminded of how bad Egypt was, believers often need to be reminded of the downside of their pre-Christian existence.

> For those who are according to the flesh set their minds on the things of the flesh. . . . For the mind set on the flesh is death . . . because the mind set on the flesh is hostile toward God; for it does not subject itself to the law of God, for it is not even able to do so, and those who are in the flesh cannot please God. (Rom. 8:5a, 6a, 7–8)

Did you catch all the elements in that grocery list? Unbelievers are characterized by:

- A *fleshly mind-set*—Non-Christians have a mental orientation toward sin. They are drawn to it like metal filings to a magnet.

- A *deadly future*—Their life leads them toward eternal separation from God.

- A *Godward hostility*—They answer to no one but themselves and violently oppose the God who requires submission.

- An *inability to obey or please God*—They have no power to change their sinful orientation, and as a result, they lack the ability to please God.

Life according to the Spirit

Life in God's Spirit, however, stands in stark contrast to the life of the flesh.

---

3. Some Christian expositors believe that this passage contrasts two types of believers—spiritual and carnal. Verse 9, which says, "You are not in the flesh but in the Spirit," seems to indicate that Paul is contrasting the Christian life with that of unbelievers.

> Those who are according to the Spirit, [set their minds on] the things of the Spirit. . . . The mind set on the Spirit is life and peace. . . .
>
> However, you are not in the flesh but in the Spirit, if indeed the Spirit of God dwells in you. But if anyone does not have the Spirit of Christ, he does not belong to Him. If Christ is in you, though the body is dead because of sin, yet the spirit is alive because of righteousness. But if the Spirit of Him who raised Jesus from the dead dwells in you, He who raised Christ Jesus from the dead will also give life to your mortal bodies through His Spirit who dwells in you. (vv. 5b, 6b, 9–11)

God's design for us is to live in a manner worthy of our new calling:

- A *spiritual orientation*—The Holy Spirit creates in us a new orientation toward righteousness, a desire to conform to Christ.

- A *peaceful existence*—The removal of God's wrath makes us His adopted sons and daughters instead of His enemies. And we can have a lasting sense of peace, knowing that we are loved by Him.

- A *Spirit-powered life*—It's often hard to imagine, but the same Spirit who physically raised Jesus Christ from the dead also spiritually empowers and enables us to lead lives that are pleasing to God.

The Disciplines of a Victorious Christian

Now that we know what the spiritual life is supposed to look like and we understand the power we've been given to conform to that picture, let's take a look at two key truths that will help us make it happen.

Resist the Flesh

From Paul's words in verses 12–13 we can develop a plan of action.

> So then, brethren, we are under obligation, not to the flesh, to live according to the flesh—for if you are living according to the flesh, you must die. (vv. 12–13a)

First, we must resist the flesh—in other words, be who we are. Paul clearly states that we are no longer of the flesh, and if we're not of the flesh, then we shouldn't live a fleshly lifestyle. As Christians, we have the ability to reject and resist it.

Live by the Spirit

Second, we should live by the Spirit.

> But if by the Spirit you are putting to death the deeds of the body, you will live. (v. 13b)

How can we live by the Spirit? And why should we? Paul tells us in Galatians that we can avoid living in the flesh by walking in the Spirit (Gal. 5:16). The more we walk in the Spirit, the more we "put to death" the deeds of the body. He also reveals a very good reason for living by the Spirit—life. Not only do we gain eternal life through our salvation, but we can "live life to the fullest" in the here and now by walking in the Spirit.

 Living Insights

Athletes have something they call "gut-check time." It's the time in every competition when the game is on the line and they're tired, swollen, and sore. Essentially, they ask themselves, "Do I have what it takes to win this game?"

When's the last time you did a spiritual gut-check, evaluating how you're doing in the Christian life? How about taking one now? You might be surprised at how well you're doing and how well equipped you are by Christ, who has given you everything you need to live for Him.

First, have you placed your trust in Christ? If so, then you can rest confidently in your salvation. Christ has met the standard of the Law for you. You don't have to earn anything to receive God's blessing of eternal life. If you have confessed your sins to God and trusted in the work of Christ, you are His child.

If you haven't trusted Christ, the following prayer is a good example of what to pray in order to do that. Remember, though, merely speaking the prayer doesn't bring salvation; it's the condition of your heart that matters.

Dear Jesus,
I need You. Thank You for dying on the cross for my sins. I now trust in Your death as the only payment for those sins. Thank You for forgiving me and giving me eternal life. Help me now as I seek to live according to Your Spirit. Amen.

Second, are you cultivating disciplines of godliness? Part of God's design for our growth is for us to develop habits that will help us reorient our mind-set to the Spirit.

Which of the following "deeds of the body" (Rom. 8:13) most easily controls your mind-set and causes you to live to fulfill those desires?

Materialism (house, car, gadgets, toys) _____

_____

_____

_____

Recognition (at work, church, other organizations, or people)

_____

_____

_____

Pleasure (leisure activities, vacations, travel) _____

_____

_____

_____

Something else? _____

_____

_____

_____

All of the above can be pursued in a normal, healthy way. There's nothing wrong with buying a nice, new sedan or desiring the admiration of your coworkers or wanting to travel to Rome.

The problem comes when we live for these things, when they control us. When we begin to sense the shift from "normal and healthy" to "fleshly," it will help to have some action steps in mind to help guide us back onto the Spirit-filled path.

How can you cultivate the following disciplines to counteract the temptations of the flesh?

Prayer _____

_____

_____

_____

Scripture memory _____

_____

_____

_____

Scripture meditation _____

_____

_____

_____

Accountability partners _____

_____

_____

_____

Chapter 5

A SPIRIT-CONTROLLED MIND-SET
Romans 8:12–17

Have you recently bought something with a credit card? If you're like millions of others, you've used your "plastic" at least once in the last twenty-four hours. And why *not*? They're so convenient; all you have to do is swipe your card through a digital machine, and *voilà*, instant purchase!

But then the day comes. You open your mailbox to find a "love letter" from your credit company, expecting you to pay for all the digital swipes you've been taking for the last thirty days.

It's payback time! Can't pay it all back right now? No problem. Just pay what you can, keep making those swipes, and, well, you'll be a steady customer for a long time—as long as you keep feeding the debt machine.

Not all debt is bad, though. Take debts of gratitude, for example. If someone pulls you out of a raging river and saves you from drowning, you'll feel indebted to that individual. You will probably want to do nice things for that person, help them out if they need it, and so on. Not because you *have* to, but because you *want* to. Because it's natural. It makes sense. It flows from your experience. From your heart.

That's the kind of indebtedness we have as Christians. We don't "owe God" in the sense that we could ever repay Him for what He's given us. But as those freed from the tyranny of the flesh and now living in the Spirit, we want to please God, to demonstrate our love for Him. Not to make us right with Him . . . but because He has made us right with Himself. That's a debt of gratitude that flows out of our regenerate hearts.

A Vital Question . . . and the Biblical Answer

Paul has made it clear in Romans that salvation is a gift from God and that we can do nothing to earn new life. Before our rebirth, we were dead in our sin, separated from God, and under His wrath. We were completely unable to earn His acceptance. Only through His mercy did God send Christ to die in our place. Through His

33

death, we were given an avenue to escape death and judgment. Our salvation was totally and completely handled by God. All we did, or could do, was receive it through faith.

Even though we're still in a sinning state, God has declared us righteous—justified us—crediting Christ's righteousness to our account.

But who handles our sanctification, the process of growing in Christ?

Many of us have bought into the idea that we're responsible for the state of our spirituality. The Lord has saved us, and now it's our job to become godly. But the Bible teaches against this view.

The biblical view is that *sanctification, just like justification, is a work of God*. We're called to cooperate with Him in the process, but we're never commanded to do it all ourselves. The Bible proves this point when it describes our purpose, empowerment, and destiny as Christians.

Our Divine Purpose

> For by grace you have been saved through faith; and that not of yourselves, it is the gift of God; not as a result of works, so that no one may boast. For we are His workmanship, created in Christ Jesus for good works, which God prepared beforehand so that we would walk in them. (Eph. 2:8–10)

We all know the first two verses, but what about verse 10? Why were we created? For good works. And who prepared those good works? God, not us.

We are *His* "workmanship," *His* work of art, *His* new creation in Christ. As the Creator, God lays before us the deeds He's crafted for us. We don't need to come up with a list of things to do on our own. Instead, we walk in the Spirit, follow His Word, and cooperate with God. As one commentator put it, "The life of goodness that regeneration produces has been prepared for believers . . . from all eternity. The road is already built."[1] God, then, superintends our sanctification.

---

1. A. Skevington Wood, "Ephesians," in *The Expositor's Bible Commentary*, gen. ed. Frank E. Gaebelein (Grand Rapids, Mich.: Zondervan Publishing House, Regency Reference Library, 1978), vol. 11, p. 36.

Our Divine Empowerment

> For I am confident of this very thing, that He who
> began a good work in you will perfect it until the
> day of Christ Jesus. (Phil. 1:6)

This, perhaps, is the clearest of all the biblical statements regarding God's role in our sanctification. Not only did God rescue us from the *penalty* of sin, but He continually rescues us from the *power* of sin. And when He glorifies us, He'll remove us from the *presence* of sin. Until then, He promises to promote our daily development in righteousness until Jesus returns. He does this by empowering us through the Holy Spirit.

Our Divine Destiny

> Now may the God of peace Himself sanctify you
> entirely; and may your spirit and soul and body be
> preserved complete, without blame at the coming of
> our Lord Jesus Christ. (1 Thess. 5:23–24)

Paul leaves no room here for us to think that sanctification is ultimately up to us. As a bride waiting for her groom, the church must be prepared for its destiny—its wedding to Christ. Upon His arrival, we must be pure and holy—"without blame." Given humanity's track record, do you think it would be wise of God to leave that task up to us? Obviously not. Therefore, He has taken it upon Himself to handle our sanctification. Just as we could not achieve our own justification, so we cannot obtain our own sanctification or glorification.

How Should We Then Live?

Since our role is to cooperate with God, how can we walk in the good works He has prepared for us? Romans 8:12–13 provides the answer, first negatively, then positively.

Not according to the Flesh

Before salvation, all human beings are bound by the flesh. They have no choice but to obey its commands—to live self-serving, self-pleasing lives. So Paul begins his comments on sanctification by describing the way salvation reorients our relationship to the flesh.

> So then, brethren, we are under obligation, not
> to the flesh, to live according to the flesh—for if
> you are living according to the flesh, you must die.
> (vv. 12–13a)

The NASB uses the word *obligation*, but the term literally means *debtor*.[2] Paul uses this word to announce that we no longer are debtors to the flesh—we no longer owe it our loyalty or obedience. Who set us free from this obligation? Who paid our balance? Jesus Christ. He paid our bill in full.

What a powerful truth! We're free—free from a lifestyle of emptiness and death that is completely contrary to the way of the Spirit of life. We now have the ability to pursue God and live in a manner worthy of the calling for which He saved us.

But to the Spirit

> But if by the Spirit you are putting to death the
> deeds of the body, you will live. (v. 13b)

Living by the Spirit is positive living, powerful and real. The Spirit helps us put to death the deadly works of the flesh. And He guides us into those good, life-giving works that "God prepared beforehand" for us (see Eph. 2:10). The key to sanctification, then, is to commit ourselves to cooperating with the Holy Spirit as He works to grow us into mature and wise believers. That cooperation is, in a sense, a debt of gratitude we pay to God for His redeeming us.

Why We Can Be Confident

Paul next explains why we can be confident of God's working on our behalf. This is essential, because "to be successful in contending against the flesh one must be assured that he has been claimed by God and equipped with his infinite resources."[3]

2. *Theological Dictionary of the New Testament*, ed. Gerhard Friedrich, translated and edited by Geoffrey W. Bromiley (1967; reprint, Grand Rapids, Mich.: William B. Eerdmans Publishing Co., 1991), vol. 5, pp. 565–66.

3. Everett F. Harrison, "Romans," in *The Expositor's Bible Commentary*, gen. ed. Frank E. Gaebelein (Grand Rapids, Mich.: Zondervan Publishing House, Regency Reference Library, 1978), vol. 10, p. 92.

We Have Been Adopted as Sons of God

> For all who are being led by the Spirit of God, these
> are sons of God. For you have not received a spirit
> of slavery leading to fear again, but you have re-
> ceived a spirit of adoption as sons by which we cry
> out, "Abba! Father!" (Rom. 8:14–15)

The Greek word for *led* in verse 14 means "to lead by laying
hold of, and this way to bring to the point of destination."[4] It was
often used to describe the way an animal is led by a harness. This
term identifies the way the Holy Spirit takes hold of us and guides
us in our Christian journey.

His leading in and of itself reassures us that we are the very
"sons of God"—a phrase that communicates our privileged position
in God's family. We have heaven's privileges, not because we were
born to them, but because God graciously chose to adopt us as His
own. He has granted us all the love, acceptance, and intimacy with
Him that He gives His own Son, Jesus Christ. That's why we can
call out, "Abba! Father!"—deeply intimate and secure terms.

Little Palestinian boys and girls addressed their fathers as
Abba—the equivalent of our word *Daddy*. This word implies a close,
loving relationship in which the child feels totally comfortable in
the presence of his or her father. How many of us love and trust
God so totally that we would rest in His arms like a toddler? As
believers, we can! God, in His great mercy, has allowed us, not only
to stand before Him, but even to sit in His lap.

We Have Been Made Children of God

> The Spirit Himself testifies with our spirit that we
> are children of God. (v. 16)

Notice that in verse 16, Paul switches from using the word *sons*
to using the word *children*. Commentator John A. Witmer notes
that here "the Holy Spirit's indwelling presence attests *the believer's
birth relationship to God*."[5] So we have not only been chosen and

---

4. James Strong, *The Exhaustive Concordance of the Bible* (Ontario, Canada: Woodside Bible
Fellowship), as cited by Logos Bible Software version 2.0a (Logos Research Systems, Inc.,
1995).

5. John A. Witmer, "Romans," in *The Bible Knowledge Commentary,* New Testament edition,
ed. John F. Walvoord and Roy B. Zuck (Colorado Springs, Colo.: Chariot Victor Publishing,
1985), p. 471.

brought into a whole new family through adoption, but we have been born anew into God's family—new creations in Christ (see 2 Cor. 5:17). And the Spirit of God delights to witness to this truth.

Satan, on the other hand, loves to plague us (especially new converts) by causing us to doubt our membership in God's family. When we continually struggle against the flesh, we can easily interpret this as a sign that our faith "didn't take." But Romans 8:16 gives us the Spirit's own assurance. For the Holy Spirit

> does not base his assuring testimony on progress or the lack of it in the Christian life. He does not lead us to cry, "I am God's child." Rather, he leads us to call upon God as Father, to look away from ourselves to him who established the relationship.[6]

We Have Been Made Heirs of God

> And if children, heirs also, heirs of God and fellow heirs with Christ, if indeed we suffer with Him so that we may also be glorified with Him. (v. 17)

Amazing! We have been offered all the riches of God, which belong to Jesus by right and will be given to us through grace. We will still suffer on earth, just as Christ suffered. That's the way of the Cross. But we will also be glorified, as Christ is now glorified, for that is our heavenly future. What better assurance can we have of our worth in God's eyes? Truly, He who began this good work in us will certainly bring it to completion!

 Living Insights

What evidence of God's work in your life have you noticed? What differences about how you live and work can you cite? Take a moment to reflect. What's different about

Whom you closely relate to (spouse, family): _____

_____

_____

6. Harrison, "Romans," p. 93.

_____

_____

Whom you know (acquaintances): _____

_____

_____

_____

_____

What you do (vocation): _____

_____

_____

_____

_____

What you own (possessions): _____

_____

_____

_____

_____

Take a moment and thank God for His faithfulness to complete the work He has begun in you (see Phil. 1:6).

Chapter 6

THE GLORY AND THE GROAN

Romans 8:16–27

Joy. Pure, unadulterated joy.

How else could you describe the way a woman feels after the birth of her child—when she holds that infant in her arms and gazes into her baby's eyes for the first time?

This greatest of all earthly joys, however, is always preceded by the greatest of all earthly pains—childbirth. Who can outdo the descriptive powers of a pregnant woman trying to explain her discomfort to the uninitiated? Words like *daggers, twisting, wringing,* and *bloating* have never been used to such graphic extent. And all this comes *before* she goes into labor! May God always protect the ears of the innocent who are within shouting distance of a woman giving birth!

So how do doctors, nurses, husbands, and other family and friends help these women endure the pain? They keep them focused on the joy to come. Often, they counsel women to have a picture or object with them to remind them of their baby. That way, when the contractions reach their peak, they'll be able to endure the suffering by anticipating the outcome.

The Christian life is a lot like pregnancy and childbirth. We've all felt bloated at times, having more of a spiritual waddle than a spiritual walk. We've all been pierced by the daggers of loss and disappointment. Every one of us has experienced the wrenching and wringing in our hearts for our unsaved friends and relatives. Yes, the Christian life does bring with it pains that have a lot in common with pregnancy. But, as Paul tells us in Romans 8:16–27, at the end of our labors are a glory and a joy so great that our pains won't even be remembered (compare John 16:21–22).

The Reality of Suffering

In the first part of this passage, Paul explains the realities associated with the "birth pains" of the Christian life.

It Is Certain

It's been said that life has two guarantees—death and taxes.

The spiritual life also has its certainties. One of those realities is suffering, and Paul doesn't skirt the issue.

> The Spirit Himself testifies with our spirit that we are children of God, and if children, heirs also, heirs of God and fellow heirs with Christ, *if indeed we suffer with Him* so that we may also be glorified with Him. (Rom. 8:16–17, emphasis added)

Don't be fooled by the use of *if* in that last phrase. We use *if* in the English language to say *perhaps* or *maybe*—to express a possibility if certain criteria are met. But the Greek phrase Paul uses here indicates a certainty; it's a synonym for the word *because*. He is telling us that we are fellow heirs with Christ *because* we suffer with Him. Suffering is a certainty in the Christian life.

In what ways have you endured tribulation? Have you experienced rejection because of your faith—maybe a family member or friend has kept you at arm's length because you became "too serious" about religion? Has a catastrophic illness changed your life? Have financial problems cornered you like a pack of snarling wolves? Have you been discriminated against because of your race, color, age, or gender?

Don't get discouraged. God knew those things would happen. He predicted them through Paul, and your sufferings are part of what makes you a fellow heir with Jesus. So, in the same way that trials are a certainty for believers in this life, so are their reward and glorification in the next life.

It Has a Purpose

If God were a sadistic killjoy, He'd throw trials in our path just to watch us squirm. And sometimes we're tempted to think that that's exactly what He does. But that's because we don't always see suffering as purposeful.

God has a specific purpose for every trial He allows. He puts obstacles in our path to strengthen, test, humble, and discipline us. But there's one more reason He allows suffering, and it's much more attractive than all the others combined—He puts us through tribulation because it leads us to glory.

Paul stated this truth explicitly when he wrote, "We suffer with Him so that we may also be glorified with Him" (v. 17b). He communicated the same idea in 2 Corinthians 4:17:

41

For momentary, light affliction is producing for us
an eternal weight of glory far beyond all comparison.
(v. 17)

Suffering has a purpose—to lead us to glory. The relationship
between earthly hardship and eternal inheritance is an important
one, as Douglas Moo notes:

> But this glorious inheritance of ours is not
> achieved apart from suffering. Because we are "one
> with" Christ, we are His fellow-heirs, assured of be-
> ing "glorified with him." But, at the same time, this
> oneness means that we must follow Christ's own road
> to glory, "suffering with him" (cf. also Phil. 1:29;
> 3:10; 2 Cor. 1:5).[1]

It Cannot Compare to Our Future

Just in case we're still tempted to drag our feet through hard
times, to focus on all the pains we're experiencing instead of trusting
in God to sustain us, Paul adds a comforting thought in the next
verse. He contrasts our present earthly trials with the heavenly joys
to come.

> For I consider that the sufferings of this present
> time are not worthy to be compared with the glory
> that is to be revealed to us. (Rom. 8:18)

As Paul points out, there is *no* comparison between our present
suffering and our future glory. From his point of view, it would be
easier to equate a sapling in your front yard to the forests of Brazil,
or a thimble of water to the Pacific Ocean. No comparison at all.
As commentator Everett F. Harrison notes,

> Weighed in the scales of true and lasting values, the
> sufferings endured in this life are light indeed, com-
> pared with the splendor of the life to come—a life
> undisturbed by anything hostile or hurtful.[2]

1. Douglas Moo, *Romans 1–8*, The Wycliffe Exegetical Commentary series (Chicago, Ill.:
Moody Press, 1991), p. 541.

2. Everett F. Harrison, "Romans," in *The Expositor's Bible Commentary*, gen. ed. Frank E.
Gaebelein (Grand Rapids, Mich.: Zondervan Publishing House, Regency Reference Library,
1976), vol. 10, pp. 93–94.

We've talked a lot about being glorified, but what exactly does that mean? In our "Key Words and Concepts in Romans" at the beginning of this guide, we've defined *glorification* as

> the consummation of salvation. It occurs, in one sense, when we die and enter the presence of the Lord. At that point we will be completely free from the presence of sin. Glorification, however, occurs at its fullest when all who have died in Christ—as well as believers who are alive at Christ's return—will receive perfect, incorruptible bodies that will last for eternity. The process of sanctification will then be complete. We will be with Jesus and like Jesus—free from the presence of sin and perfect in body and soul.

Now that's a hope that can keep us going! Let's try to emulate Paul in our attitude and outlook toward suffering. But how can we adopt a godly view of our illnesses, financial troubles, broken relationships, and difficulties at work, church, and home? Fortunately, Paul himself shows us how in the next four verses by identifying four facts about suffering.

Four Facts about Suffering

In Paul's next four verses, he reminds us that we're not alone in longing to end the groan and get to glory—the whole creation suffers along with us. From this illustration of parallel yearning we can take away four helpful reminders.

First, *"groaning" is temporary.*

> For the anxious longing of the creation waits eagerly
> for the revealing of the sons of God. (v. 19)

Between the lines of this verse is an encouraging truth: suffering and dying are not permanent but only temporary. A bright, new *eternal* world is waiting to be revealed.

Did you catch the words "anxiously longing" and "waits eagerly"? J. B. Phillips phrased this as "the whole creation is on tiptoe"—straining to see what we Christians, "sons of God," will be in our glorified state. John A. Witmer explains that the Greek verb for "waits eagerly," *apekdechomai*, is used seven times in the New Testament, each time to refer to Christ's return (Rom. 8:19, 23, 25; 1 Cor. 1:7; Gal. 5:5; Phil. 3:20; Heb. 9:28). The revealing of the sons of God will occur when Christ returns for His own. They will share His glory . . . and will be transformed. . . . All of nature (inanimate and animate) is personified as waiting eagerly for that time.[3]

How's your anticipation factor? Are you as eager as the rest of creation to see your final and complete redemption? Do you daydream about heaven? Are you waiting for Jesus on your tiptoes with a craned neck, like a child peering at the fireplace on Christmas Eve night?

If we'll consistently remind ourselves of the glory to come, we can endure suffering. The sour tinge of suffering will give way to the sweet and savory taste of glory.

Second, *"groaning" is a consequence of the Fall.*

> For the creation was subjected to futility, not willingly, but because of Him who subjected it. (v. 20a)

Paul is referring here to the cursing of the earth in Genesis 3:17, in which God said to Adam, "Cursed is the ground because of you." The Garden of Eden never experienced a forest fire, earthquake, mud slide, flood, or tornado. No hurricanes, blizzards, or heat waves; no locust plagues or rat infestations. It was a perfect paradise devoid of any physical, emotional, or spiritual pain. Until Adam and Eve sinned against God. Ever since then, all of nature has been subjected to frustration, that is, borne the pain of human disobedience to God. All suffering, then, is a consequence of the Fall, which God allows in His sovereignty . . . with a certain end in view.

Third, *"groaning" is a means to an end.*

> In hope that the creation itself also will be set free from its slavery to corruption into the freedom of the glory of the children of God. (vv. 20b–21)

Why did God allow all of creation to suffer because of human

3. John A. Witmer, "Romans," in *The Bible Knowledge Commentary*, New Testament edition, ed. John F. Walvoord and Roy B. Zuck (Colorado Springs, Colo.: Chariot Victor Publishing, 1983), p. 472.

sin? Because God had an end in mind: our deliverance from sin's slavery. And once God's children realize that freedom, experience the consummation of redemption, so will creation. As our sin enslaved creation to decay and death, so our glorification at Christ's coming will result in creation's freedom.

Have you ever thought about what creation's cycle of decay-death-birth-growth-decay-death-and-so-on is here for? Not only does it remind us of the transient, fleeting nature of life in general, but it is constantly in our faces about our own brief time on this earth. Also, it keeps us uncomfortable. We're a stubborn race. Without pain, we would never feel the need to be saved. Without a judgment passed against us, we'd never know we had transgressed God's standards. In this sense, we're like sheep—we need to be prodded by pain for our own safety. The pain of living in a cursed world pushes us toward Christ. And our hope of ultimate redemption and a renewed world helps us endure.

Finally, *"groaning" is universal.*

> For we know that the whole creation groans and suffers the pains of childbirth together until now. (v. 22)

Not only is suffering as painful as childbirth, it's also universal—no one, and no part of creation, is exempt. But just as the pains of childbirth are quickly forgotten once the newborn arrives, so will our pain disappear when we pass into glory. For now, though, we live in that age when redemption has begun but is not yet complete.

How, then, can we cultivate a godly perspective on suffering? By remembering that it is temporary and that it draws us closer to Christ . . . and that it will end forever when we finally see Him face-to-face.

The Response to Suffering

In the final verses of our study, we can find practical help for responding to trials.

Groaning and Longing

First, Paul reveals that our response to suffering is similar to creation's.

> And not only this, but also we ourselves, having the

45

first fruits of the Spirit,[4] even we ourselves groan within ourselves, waiting eagerly for our adoption as sons, the redemption of our body. (v. 23)

Paul elaborates on this groaning caused by the tension between our present existence and our future reality in his second letter to the Corinthians. There he uses the metaphor of a tent to signify our earthly bodies and a heavenly dwelling to represent our immortal bodies.

> Now we know that if the earthly tent we live in is destroyed, we have a building from God, an eternal house in heaven, not built by human hands. Meanwhile we groan, longing to be clothed with our heavenly dwelling, because when we are clothed, we will not be found naked. For while we are in this tent, we groan and are burdened, because we do not wish to be unclothed but to be clothed with our heavenly dwelling, so that what is mortal may be swallowed up by life. (2 Cor. 5:1–4 NIV)

Fortunately, our groanings are like those of a pregnant woman—painful in the present but with the hope of a glorious outcome. The pregnant woman receives her baby; we will receive our heavenly inheritance.

Hoping and Waiting

> For in hope we have been saved, but hope that is seen is not hope; for who hopes for what he already sees? But if we hope for what we do not see, with perseverance we wait eagerly for it. (Rom. 8:24–25)

Unlike other people, Christians have a source of strength from which to draw during hard times. We know that no matter what trials life holds for us, our eternal destiny will be one of pleasure and security. In other words, we have hope.

All too often, however, we Christians lose sight of that hope.

---

4. "The first fruits of the Spirit" is a phrase rich in meaning. As John Witmer explains, "A farmer's 'firstfruits' were the initial harvesting of his first-ripened crops. This first installment was a foretaste and promise that more harvest was to come. Similarly God the Holy Spirit, indwelling believers, is a foretaste that they will enjoy many more blessings, including living in God's presence forever." "Romans," *The Bible Knowledge Commentary*, p. 472.

We so easily slip into the world's way of thinking, which says, "If I can't see it, I won't believe it." But Paul reminds us that hope based on things we can see is not hope at all. His words encourage us to trust God—to believe in what we can't see. When we do that, we develop the ability to persevere through hard times because we're putting more stock into our future life in heaven than into our present life on earth.

Praying and Searching

Finally, Paul describes how the Holy Spirit helps us persevere in our suffering.

> In the same way the Spirit also helps our weakness; for we do not know how to pray as we should, but the Spirit Himself intercedes for us with groanings too deep for words; and He who searches the hearts knows what the mind of the Spirit is, because he intercedes for the saints according to the will of God. (vv. 26–27)

Creation groans. We groan. Even the Holy Spirit groans—that is, He prays for us to the Father when we're in too much pain to voice our own needs. Like when we lose our loved ones or possessions. When we're numbed by tragedy. When we don't even have the strength to look heavenward.

In those times, we are not alone. The Holy Spirit stands in the gap and speaks to the Father for us when we don't know what to say. And not only that, but His prayers for us are always aligned with the will of God.

Taking Glory in the Groan

Wouldn't it be great if we could do more than simply endure or escape suffering like the rest of the world? To see it as purposeful? To walk through it with a sense of security and a sure hope of our future? And think of the implications: we'd please God with our eternal perspective, and we'd testify to the world about the difference God has made in our lives.

We can do all this and more . . . by taking Paul's words to heart. The groan, as we've seen, is only half the story. Because of Christ, we have the glory of eternity to look forward to, as William Barclay notes.

The Christian is involved in the human situation. Within he must battle with his own evil human nature; without he must live in a world of death and decay. Nonetheless, the Christian does not live only in the world; he also lives in Christ. He does not see only the world; he looks beyond it to God. He does not see only the consequences of man's sin; he sees the power of God's mercy and love. Therefore, the keynote of the Christian life is always hope and never despair. The Christian waits, not for death, but for life.[5]

Living Insights

Take a moment to consider the sufferings you've endured in the past and how they've shaped your spiritual life.

Identify the landmark trials that have come your way.

_____

_____

_____

_____

_____

_____

From what perspective did you view those challenges; that is, did your future hope help light your way through suffering's darkness?

_____

_____

_____

5. William Barclay, The Letter to the Romans, rev. ed., The Daily Study Bible Series (Philadelphia, Pa.: Westminster Press, 1975), p. 111.

How has your attitude during times of suffering impacted your overall spiritual health?

_____

_____

_____

_____

_____

None of us wants to think about the hard times that may lie ahead, but the truth is, most of us will encounter challenges in the future. Pregnant women take whole courses to prepare for childbirth. Why shouldn't we prepare for our future pains as well?

Take a moment to remind yourself of God's view of suffering. Remember that it's only temporary and always has a purpose. Finally, hope in the Lord and wait for Him to provide for you and sustain you.

Chapter 7

PROVIDENCE MADE PRACTICAL

Romans 8:28–30

Can you imagine how nails might feel?

If they could talk, those spiky splines would tell tales of malicious treatment and horrendous beatings at the hands of bullies who are much larger and harder than they. Yes, to them a hammer must seem like a brutal, merciless assailant who lives to pound them into submission, to beat them down out of sight and into permanent wooden graves. And from those graves, they could only be freed by being tortuously wrenched and possibly deformed.

What a life! It's certainly not an easy one.

And neither is ours.

How many times have we felt like poor, pathetic nails—pounded and driven between a rock and hard place by situations beyond our control? Sometimes it seems like we're unable to do anything but take the beating and live with the debilitating effects.

What can we do? There's no place to hide from life's hard times, and no one has ever been able to—not even the apostle Paul. Especially not Paul. He was arrested, beaten with rods, and thrown into prison with his feet locked in stocks. He had friends who betrayed him and ailments that crippled him. He suffered through shipwrecks and dangerous missionary expeditions. He was a "pain magnet" if there ever was one. If Paul were a nail, he'd be the most tortured one in the whole bucket.

And if there was ever a person who could justifiably resist and resent life's pain, Paul was it. He was a good man who didn't "deserve" so many trials. Many of us would have responded with anger and bitterness, had we been in Paul's shoes. But he didn't react that way. Instead, he received and learned to rejoice in what God placed in his path.

Can we live like that? Can we do more than just grudgingly

This chapter includes material from Chuck's message "Providence Made Personal" in the Living Insights section.

endure life? Can we live it to the fullest in spite of its difficulties? From Romans 8:28–30, we'll see that we can—by recognizing God's providence, His control over all events.

Understanding providence helps us put life's highs and lows into a godly perspective. Otherwise, we're destined to view hardships as enemies and, as a result, end up like nails on the scrap heap, twisted and broken by our own bitterness and resentment. With God's help, though, we can see trials as a positive force. We can stand straight and strong and become useful implements for God as He builds His kingdom here on earth.

Wrestling against God's Providence

What precisely do we mean when we speak of God's providence? *The New Bible Dictionary* defines it as

> the unceasing activity of the Creator whereby, in overflowing bounty and goodwill . . . he upholds his creatures in ordered existence . . . guides and governs all events, circumstances and free acts of angels and men . . . and directs everything to its appointed goal, for his own glory.[1]

And what specifically does that mean for Christians?

> That the events of our lives are not ruled by chance or fate but by our sovereign God and loving Lord who works out His plan and purpose in the lives of all His children. . . . It also speaks of God's gracious provision and care for our daily needs.[2]

God's providence can be a source of great reassurance and comfort, yet we often struggle with it. Why? One reason is that we have trouble reconciling "God is love" with "God guides and governs *all* events"—including the painful, hard, and unjust ones. For example, why would a good God allow a child to be abused? Another reason we struggle against God's providence is our aversion to being controlled. Several other reasons come to mind as well.

1. J. I. Packer, "Providence," in the *New Bible Dictionary*, 2d ed. (1982; reprint, Downers Grove, Ill.: InterVarsity Press, 1991), p. 990.

2. *The Living Insights Study Bible*, gen. ed. Charles R. Swindoll (Grand Rapids, Mich.: Zondervan Publishing House, 1996), p. 1423.

- **Selfishness.** When God places difficulties in our path, like financial troubles or personal loss, our first response is usually, "Why me, Lord?" Not that we really want to know His reasons or how our suffering might glorify Him. Rather, we want to know why He's blocking our way. Our question is really a complaint against all the discomfort and discouragement He's causing us. It's a cry for Him to get out of our way so we can "do our own thing"—pursue wealth, collect possessions . . . whatever.

- **Fear.** We cherish our lives and dreams, and the thought of relinquishing the control of those things to others—especially God—frightens us. We've all wondered, *What if God wants me to become a missionary in Africa and live with huge snakes and bugs? What if God doesn't want me to have the things that I want—a home of my own, a spouse, children? What if God wants to take my health?* Human nature makes self-preservation our top priority.

- **Pride.** "God has given us free will, so why shouldn't we use it?" pride asks. "We're not puppets on a string! We've got minds of our own!" True. We are not robots programmed to impassionately do God's bidding. But we are sheep who need the guidance and discipline of a Good Shepherd who will lead us in the way that's best for us and for His purposes. That's humbling . . . a blow to our "I can do it on my own" mentality.

At the root of all these reasons seems to be the doubt that God is really good, that He can really be trusted. If that is at the core of why you sometimes struggle with God's providence, Paul has reassuring news for you in Romans 8:28–30.

The Nature of Providence

Paul begins by describing the nature of God's control.

> And we know that God causes all things to work together for good to those who love God, to those who are called according to His purpose. (v. 28)

If we break this verse into four parts, we can better grasp its meaning and mine its riches.

The Promise Is Based on Fact, Not Feeling

First, Paul reminds the Roman believers that they *knew* about God's providence: "And we *know* that . . ." The Greek phrase used here for *know that, oidamen hoti*, describes a known fact—something we can have an unshakable confidence in, despite our circumstances or feelings.[3]

Paul wants to remind us to trust in God and His plan in hard times. When it seems like He's a thousand miles away, we don't need to wonder or guess if He's with us. He is, and all events work together for our ultimate good. We *know* that He is in control, regardless of what we think or feel. So let's remember what we already *know* of God through the history revealed in the Scriptures.

The Project Is God's, Not Ours

"And we know that God *causes* . . ." Who controls everything? God does. Not us, not nature. God orchestrates history. What a comforting thought! If we were in control, humanity would be headed for certain destruction. If nature were in control, our prognosis wouldn't be much better. But the Lord is at the helm of history, steering the ship toward His divine purpose.

He is the potter, we are the clay (see Jer. 18:1–6). The potter is in charge, and the clay is in process. We can take comfort that God superintends every situation. Even when we suffer, He can make something useful of it. Be encouraged. Since God is in control, He will accomplish His purposes in our lives.

God's Plan Is Total, Not Partial

"And we know that God causes *all things* to work together . . ." Do you think Paul meant to say "most things"? Surely there are actions and consequences that God cannot or will not use for our good. Infidelity, for example. Or what about the hurricanes that hit the Gulf Coast every year? Certainly He would have a hard time squeezing any good out of those tragedies.

Sins, natural disasters—we tend to see these as our enemies, our hammers. But God often uses them to turn us toward Him. God hates sin, but once it has been committed, He can use it for good. God hates death and pain, but He can use it to have a powerful, positive influence on people. Yes, God can and does use *all things* for our good. We may not see the good in it right away—or ever in this life. We may not be able to put all the pieces of the puzzle

3. James D. G. Dunn, *Romans 1–8*, Word Biblical Commentary Series (Dallas, Tex.: Word Books, Publisher, 1988), vol. 38, pp. 80, 480.

together. But because we are in Christ, we can assess all of life as somehow beneficial to our maturing in Him.

God's Purpose Is Good, Not Evil

"And we know that God causes all things to work together *for good* . . ." Notice, the verse doesn't say that all things will *feel* good. It doesn't say that they will *seem* good. It doesn't even say that all things *are* good. But it does tell us that they will work together *for* His children's good.

And it's important to note that this promise applies only to Christians. As Paul made clear in the balance of this verse, "And we know that God causes all things to work together for good *to those who love God, to those who are called according to His purpose*" (emphasis added). As John Stott notes,

> This is a necessary limitation. Paul is not expressing a general, superficial optimism that everything tends to everybody's good in the end. No, if the "good" which is God's objective is our completed salvation, then its beneficiaries are his people who are described as those who love him.[4]

Ultimately, we have to trust that God loves us and wants the best for us. We're "called according to His purpose." He didn't save us and then leave us to fend for ourselves. Our redemption, our whole life, fits into His eternal plan. Knowing that will keep us from seeing hardship as a random mess. If we doubt His benevolence, suspicion will creep into every trouble we face, plaguing our spiritual lives.

Faith is the antidote to doubt. And while the Bible tells us to walk by faith and not by sight, we should not walk as though we were completely blind. Our faith is not groundless. We have the proof of Christ who lived in the flesh and died on the cross to redeem us while we were still living in rebellion against God. He suffered more than we ever will, and He did it because He loves us. His purpose is good—good for us as well as for His glory.

---

4. John Stott, *Romans: God's Good News for the World* (Downers Grove, Ill.: InterVarsity Press, 1994), p. 247.

The Purpose of Providence

Now that we've equipped ourselves with four comforting truths about providence, let's look at how God accomplishes His "purpose" (v. 28).

> For those whom He foreknew,[5] He also predestined to become conformed to the image of His Son, so that He would be the firstborn among many brethren; and these whom He predestined, He also called; and these whom He called, He also justified; and these whom He justified, He also glorified. (vv. 29–30)

These verse provide, first, a model, and second, a process that conforms us to that model.

The Model

God orchestrates events in order to conform us to the image of Christ. Jesus is the pattern; Christlikeness is the goal. Everything we go through—the disasters that ravage our lives, the consequences of our choices, the people who impact us for good and bad—is used by God to shape us into Christ's image. Then we will be Christ's brothers and sisters, not just in name, but in actual "family resemblance" (see v. 29). As John A. Witmer explains,

> By all saints being made like Christ (ultimate and complete sanctification), Christ will be exalted as the Firstborn among many brothers. The resurrected and glorified Lord Jesus Christ will become the Head of a new race of humanity purified from all contact with sin and prepared to live eternally in His presence (cf. 1 Cor. 15:42–49). As the "Firstborn" He is in the highest position among others (cf. Col. 1:18).[6]

5. The term *foreknew* conveys love and warmth. Commentator John A. Witmer adds that it "does not mean simply that God foreknows *what* believers will do, but that God foreknows *them*. Nor does divine foreknowledge merely mean an awareness of or acquaintance with an individual. Instead it means a meaningful relationship with a person based on God's choice (cf. Jer. 1:4–5; Amos 3:2) in eternity before Creation." "Romans," *The Bible Knowledge Commentary*, New Testament edition, ed. John F. Walvoord and Roy B. Zuck (Colorado Spring, Colo.: Chariot Victor Publishing, 1983), p. 474.

6. Witmer, "Romans," p. 474.

Knowing God's plan for the future must have helped Paul remain content no matter what his circumstances (see Phil. 4:11). To Paul, there was purpose in both life's joy—and its pain. He believed that every trial was just another blow of the sculptor's chisel, knocking away the sin and hard edges from his life in order to fashion him into the likeness of the Savior.

The Process

Conformity to Christ's image—that's sanctification. But is that the only stage of salvation over which God exerts control? No, says Paul. God also predestined us, called us, justified us, and will glorify us.[7] From His first thought to choose us to the day we stand in His presence, our salvation is the work of God and rests secure in His sovereign hands.

Some theologians of the past have reduced the content of verse 30 to a dry, five-step recipe for glorification. But Paul meant it as a lyrical expression of the Christian experience. No matter what we make of the five elements identified here by Paul, we can rest assured of one fact—God possesses providential control over our lives from start to finish. He knew us before we were born, before the foundations of the earth were even laid. And He accompanies us every step of the way—all the way into heaven.

Responding to Providence

Life's hammers will pound us. Sicknesses will come, and friends will leave. Pressures will build, and pain will visit us. The difference between standing strong and falling to pieces lies in how we view those hammers.

Will we see them as malevolent enemies who only want to drive us into wooden graves? Or will we remind ourselves that they are tools in God's hands, designed to conform us to Christ's image so we can advance His kingdom here on earth? He, the Master Craftsman, knows what He's doing. So let's yield to the hammers without complaint so that God can work in us and for us and through us.

---

7. Though glorification is yet future for us, Paul writes of it in the present tense in order to emphasize its certainty.

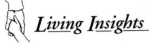 *Living Insights*

W. Graham Scroggie once wrote, "The New [Testament] is in the Old contained, and the Old is in the New explained."[8] In other words, many of the principles taught by New Testament writers were illustrated by Old Testament characters. Take Joseph, for example.

As a teen, Joseph was seized by his brothers, thrown into a pit, and sold into slavery. For almost two dozen years, he lived in Egypt—maligned, misjudged, imprisoned, and betrayed. But because God's hand was on Joseph, he eventually rose to a place of prominence in his new land. When he saw his brothers again—after a famine forced them to travel into Egypt for food—Joseph responded in a way that only a providence-minded man could have. Instead of destroying their lives as they had tried to do to his, he forgave them.

Why was Joseph able to respond in love to such a horrible act? Because he realized that God had sovereignly used it to bring about a greater good in His plan. Because he viewed his circumstances—good and bad—from God's perspective, he never became bitter but rather lived in a state of confidence in God's control.

Compared to a person like Joseph, we tend to feel inadequate. But he was just as human as we are. We can trust in God's providence too. Take a few moments to make providence practical in your life by answering the following questions.

When have you wrestled with God's providence? Be specific; describe the circumstances and identify the ways in which you reacted . . .

out of selfishness: _____

_____

_____

_____

8. W. Graham Scroggie, *Know Your Bible*, p. 12; as quoted by Norman L. Geisler and William E. Nix, in *A General Introduction to the Bible*, revised and expanded (Chicago, Ill.: Moody Press, 1986), p. 22.

out of fear: _____

_____

_____

_____

out of pride: _____

_____

_____

How about the times you responded to providence with trust? Describe the situation and how your perspective helped your walk with the Lord.

_____

_____

_____

_____

_____

_____

If Christlikeness is our goal, and if remembering and relying on God's providence is one way to move toward that goal, identify ways in which you can help yourself rest in God's control on a daily basis.

_____

_____

_____

_____

_____

_____

Chapter 8

WE OVERWHELMINGLY CONQUER

Romans 8:31–39

Pop quiz! Now, now, mop those beads of sweat from your forehead. There'll be no oral exam, no grade, no future career at stake. Just two questions for you to answer. Ready?

1. What's the most dangerous ideology in the world?

Stop and think a moment. Don't answer too quickly; the best answer may not be the first one that comes to mind.

Is it communism? Nazism? Satanism? Without a doubt, these belief systems are menacing and hazardous to humanity. But can any one of them be considered the *most* dangerous?

Maybe, but another ideology can create even more problems. Its name? Humanism. That's right, humanism—the philosophy that sparked the Renaissance. The ideology that brought light to the so-called Dark Ages of the medieval period and that encouraged people to rediscover the great literature of antiquity, of Greece and Rome.

Humanism has brought a lot of good to civilization, but it comes with a sly danger. Celebrating human capabilities, such as learning and enlightenment, it can blind us to our need for God. Claiming that "man is the measure of all things,"[1] it praises what it views as the indomitable, unconquerable nature of the human spirit—leaving little room in the heart for God, and no place for His omniscience and power.

Surprisingly, humanism has even slipped into the church. People tend to emphasize what they do for God instead of what God has done for them. They go to church every time the doors open. They give up things. They try to be perfect. In short, they adopt a works mentality and lose sight of the gospel. Humanism, then, may very well be the most accurate answer to our first question, because it can subvert the Christian faith like no other ideology can.

---

1. The Greek philosopher Protagoras, as quoted in *The Dictionary of Cultural Literacy*, by E. D. Hirsch Jr., Joseph F. Kett, and James Trefil (New York, N.Y.: Houghton Mifflin Co., 1993), p. 98. The humanists of the Renaissance, as part of their love for Greek philosophy, integrated this idea into their own ideology.

Let's move on to the next question.

2. What is the most powerful creature living on earth today?

A grizzly bear? An elephant? A lion? How about an angry gorilla? Not even close. According to Paul in Romans 8, it's a sheep.

You're probably wondering how he came up with *that* answer, and what humanism and sheep have to do with each other. (And who came up with these questions, anyway!)

Well, to be truthful, sheep are the most powerful creatures only metaphorically speaking. Psalm 100:3 says that we are the sheep of God's pasture, and in Romans 8:37, Paul says that because we sheep have God on our side, we "overwhelmingly conquer" (v. 37). Here's where the link to humanism comes in—it's only by the grace of God—not our own strength and work and knowledge and enlightenment—that we are truly indomitable. The love of God is limitless in its power, but the human spirit is hemmed in by limits on all sides.

Well, the quiz is over. Let's join our teacher, Paul, to discover the power humanism hides and learn how we, as sheep, can conquer anything because of God's love.

Paul's Questions

Verses 31–35 of chapter 8 are structured around six questions posed by Paul.

What Then Shall We Say?

What then shall we say to these things?
(Rom. 8:31a)

What "things" is Paul referring to? To the truths in the previous three verses (vv. 28–30), namely:

- the providence of God;

- His ability to make all things work together for the good of those who love Him;

- and His divine plan to predestine all believers to be like Christ by foreknowing, calling, justifying, and one day glorifying them.

Do we achieve these through anything in ourselves? Absolutely not. Remember, Jesus didn't come to make bad people good; He came to bring dead people to life! The only thing that can make us conquering sheep is the Spirit of God, who is provided by God's grace.

Who Shall Oppose Us?

With his next question, Paul provides us with one of the best descriptions of grace.

> If God is for us, who is against us? (v. 31b)

God is for us—four monosyllabic words that spell out *grace*. The word *if* at the beginning of the phrase would be better translated *since* or *because*. So the question could be rephrased, "Since God is for us, who can be against us?" But Paul isn't really asking a question, is he? No, he's actually making a bold statement—"Since God is for us, no one can be against us!"

That's a powerful truth! In a world full of suffering and groaning, in a world filled with enemies, the God of the universe stands on our side. Armed with this truth, the people of God have nothing to fear from this world (see Ps. 27:1; 56:4).

Some of us, however, wrongly fear that God Himself is against us, that He's angry with us. So Paul points out just how much God is for us.

> He who did not spare His own Son, but delivered Him over for us all, how will He not also with Him freely give us all things? (Rom. 8:32)

God didn't even spare His own Son for our sake. Stop and let that sink in. Let the grace and love of that act embrace you. Having willingly paid the ultimate price with His Son, won't God most certainly continue to freely lavish on us His continuing, unfailing generosity?

Who Shall Accuse Us?

Now that Paul has established the fact that God, being "for us," will give us anything and everything we need, he starts fleshing out some of the specific provisions the Lord gives to His people. The first is protection from accusation:

> Who will bring a charge against God's elect? God is the one who justifies. (v. 33)

Who accuses Christians? We might do better to ask, who *doesn't* accuse Christians? Satan certainly does (Rev. 12:10). The world does also (John 15:18–21). We Christians even accuse ourselves, carrying around a sense of guilt and shame when we blow it—even if our standards are hopelessly perfectionistic.

God, however, doesn't accuse His people. He has, in fact, already declared us justified, so any accusations that come against us—whether from Satan, the world, or even ourselves—lack any power or authority. The Judge has spoken, He has declared us righteous, and His word is final.

Who Shall Condemn Us?

Since no one has the authority to accuse God's people, then certainly no one has the power to condemn us either:

> Who is the one who condemns? Christ Jesus is He who died, yes, rather who was raised, who is at the right hand of God, who also intercedes for us. (Rom. 8:34)

Jesus Christ is the only Person who has been given the position to judge humankind (John 5:22, 27; Acts 17:31). And yet He's the very One who died for us, who rose again so that we might rise with Him, and who intercedes on our behalf. To the unbeliever, Christ is a judge. But to the believer, He's an advocate—a lawyer for the defense. He would never condemn those for whom He died.

It's a shame, then, that so many Christians are afraid of God. They walk through life trying to avoid Him because they feel unworthy. They think their lack of perfection gives them no right to stand in His presence. But the One they fear the most, they should fear the least. God has rendered His judgment, and the verdict is in: "Not guilty." Grace nullifies opposition; grace silences accusations; grace overrules condemnation. The case has been closed, never to be reopened. No one shall condemn us, not even God. He waits for each of us with open arms.

Who Shall Separate Us?

Paul fleshes out one final benefit of God's being "for us":

> Who will separate us from the love of Christ? Will tribulation, or distress, or persecution, or famine, or nakedness, or peril, or sword? (Rom. 8:35)

Who might separate Christians from their Lord? An opponent might try, but if God Himself is for us, that ultimately takes the power out of any opposition. Also, an accusation leading to condemnation cannot separate us from God, because He has already dealt with our guilt. We've seen that no one can accuse or condemn a believer.

Paul affirms that nothing can drive a wedge between God and His people, no matter how painful or hard things might be. He knew this from experience (see 2 Cor. 11:23–28). But for any who still wonder, he elaborates with a list of possibilities that increase in severity.

He begins with "tribulation": hard circumstances that press down on us. Then he moves to "distress": situations that confine and oppress us with their narrowness—we could phrase this as being in "dire straits." Next is "persecution": times when we are pursued by people intent on our harm. Then comes "famine": a helpless hunger brought on by drought, crop failure, earthquakes, floods, fires, swarms of locusts, or war. Next is "nakedness": poverty so harsh that a person can't afford needed clothing. Paul then advances to "peril": being in danger of arrest, false trial and imprisonment, attack, beatings, even of being killed. Which is what "sword" means: Christians executed or murdered for their faith, as James was in Acts 12:2.[2]

How easily we mistake such circumstances for a sign of God's judgment, displeasure, anger, or abandonment. But Paul assures us that none of these situations separates us from His *love*. Commentator Everett F. Harrison asks and answers a key question.

> Can there conceivably be a contradiction between Christ's love for his own and his allowing suffering to overtake them? Should the saints question whether Christ's love has grown cold? Severance from his love is no more thinkable than that the Father ceased to love his Son when he allowed him to endure the agonies of the cross, apparently forsaken. Christ predicted trouble for his people who are left in the world, but told them to be of good cheer because he had overcome the world (John 16:33). . . . Whereas the people of God in the OT were often perplexed about the reason for their trials, the saints of NT times can trace their sufferings back to identification with Christ and rejoice that they are counted worthy to suffer for his name (cf. Acts 5:41).[3]

2. See James Montgomery Boice, *Romans, Volume 2: The Reign of Grace (Romans 5–8)* (Grand Rapids, Mich.: Baker Book House, 1992), pp. 985–88.

3. Everett F. Harrison, "Romans," in *The Expositor's Bible Commentary*, gen. ed. Frank E. Gaebelein (Grand Rapids, Mich.: Zondervan Publishing House, Regency Reference Library, 1976), vol. 10, p. 99.

Overwhelming Conquerors

In this context of suffering and persecution, Paul didn't want to belittle suffering and the feelings it causes. He had been in some very dangerous and dark circumstances himself. He'd been beaten for his faith many times, almost to the point of death. He'd found himself in shipwrecks and wild rivers as a result of his faith, almost losing his life more than once. Paul had seen suffering face-to-face, and he knew that it could cause very real pain and despair. So he quotes Psalm 44:22, which reminds his readers that God's people have always borne the pain of the world's hostility:

> Just as it is written,
>> "For Your sake we are being put to death all day
>> long:
>> We were considered as sheep to be slaughtered."
> (Rom. 8:36)

Death! Paul knew that suffering could feel like death, or leave the sufferer wishing for it. The death referred to in this passage, though, was not the honorable demise of valiant warriors who go down fighting. No, this was the humiliating ruin of helpless people who had no means to defend themselves—like sheep led to the slaughter. As John A. Witmer notes,

> In the early days of the church one or more Christians were martyred every day, or faced the possibility of it. Their persecutors valued Christians' lives as nothing more than animals to be butchered.[4]

Thankfully, death isn't the end of the story:

> But in all these things we overwhelmingly conquer through Him who loved us. (v. 37)

Wow, what a turnaround! From helpless sheep to overwhelming conquerors! How is such a transformation possible? Only through the God who loves us. We conquer this world only by trusting, not in our own efforts, but in God, who provides us with the courage and strength we need to persevere.

---

4. John A. Witmer, "Romans," in *The Bible Knowledge Commentary*, New Testament edition, ed. John F. Walvoord and Roy B. Zuck (Colorado Springs, Colo.: Chariot Victor Publishing, 1983), p. 475.

When we learn this secret of our spiritual power—resting in the love of God—we develop the confidence of Paul, which is revealed in the final, climactic words of chapter 8:

> For I am convinced that neither death, nor life, nor angels, nor principalities, nor things present, nor things to come, nor powers, nor height, nor depth, nor any other created thing, will be able to separate us from the love of God, which is in Christ Jesus our Lord. (vv. 38–39)

This love of God makes us overwhelming conquerors, as Charles Wesley so eloquently expressed in his hymn "Earth, Rejoice, Our Lord Is King!"

> Earth, rejoice, our Lord is King!
>   Sons of men, His praises sing;
> Sing ye in triumphant strains,
>   Jesus the Messiah reigns!
>
> Power is all to Jesus given,
>   Lord of hell, and earth, and heaven,
> Every knee to Him shall bow;
>   Satan, hear, and tremble now!
>
> Angels and archangels join,
>   All triumphantly combine,
> All in Jesu's praise agree,
>   Carrying on His victory.
>
> Though the sons of night blaspheme,
>   More there are with us than them;
> God with us, we cannot fear;
>   Fear, ye fiends, for Christ is here!
>
> Lo, to faith's enlightened sight,
>   All the mountain flames with light!
> Hell is nigh, but God is nigher,
>   Circling us with hosts of fire.
>
> Christ the Saviour is come down,
>   Points us to the victor's crown,
> Bids us take our seats above,
>   More than conquerors in His love.

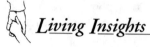 *Living Insights*

We've come a long way in our study of Romans, haven't we? Think about where we began. In the beginning, we ran into troubling verses like these:

> For the wrath of God is revealed from heaven against all ungodliness and unrighteousness of men who suppress the truth in unrighteousness. (1:18)

> There will be tribulation and distress for every soul of man who does evil, of the Jew first and also of the Greek. (2:9)

These verses are troubling because they apply to *us*, not just to mass murderers. Later in our journey, we learned the uplifting truth that we could avoid God's judgment through faith in Christ. However, another fact brought us down again—that our flesh continues to hold sway over our bodies. Paul noted:

> I see a different law in the members of my body, waging war against the law of my mind and making me a prisoner of the law of sin which is in my members. Wretched man that I am! Who will set me free from the body of this death? (7:23–24)

Once again, we found ourselves in a valley—a valley shared by the whole of creation (8:20, 22). Yes, we've come a long way, and the road hasn't always been easy. But now, at the pinnacle of Romans 8:31–39, we're on top of the mountain. We know that we are conquerors with God!

In the next chapter, however, we'll find ourselves challenged to grapple with the hard mysteries of God's sovereignty and human responsibility—a tough and often rocky climb.

Before we leave this peak, then, let's solidify in our hearts and minds the reliance on God that will sustain us throughout the rest of our journey. Let's commit ourselves to live as conquerors, to trust in God for everything we need—every word, every action, every thought, every ounce of energy. Here's a prayer to help us, which was first spoken by a true conqueror:

> I arise today
> Through God's strength to pilot me:

God's might to uphold me,
God's wisdom to guide me,
God's eye to look before me,
God's ear to hear me,
God's word to speak for me,
God's hand to guard me,
God's way to lie before me,
God's shield to protect me,
God's host to save me,
From snares of devils,
From temptations of vices,
From everyone who shall wish me ill,
Afar and anear,
Alone and in multitude. . . .

Christ to shield me today
Against poison, against burning,
Against drowning, against wounding,
So that there may come to me abundance of reward.
Christ with me, Christ before me, Christ behind me,
Christ in me, Christ beneath me, Christ above me,
Christ on my right, Christ on my left,
Christ when I lie down, Christ when I sit down,
Christ when I arise.[5]

May we go forward secure in the Lord's love and nearness. See you on the other side of the mountain!

---

5. St. Patrick's Breastplate prayer, as quoted by Thomas Cahill, in *How the Irish Saved Civilization* (New York, N.Y.: Doubleday, Bantam Doubleday Dell Publishing Group, 1995), pp. 116–19.

Chapter 9

GOD, THE JEW, AND YOU TOO

Romans 9–11

Driving can really test your focusing skills.

Have you ever been cruising down a long stretch of familiar road, when suddenly you noticed that the surroundings weren't so familiar? What had happened? Had you drifted into the wrong lane and exited too early? Or maybe passed the exit you were supposed to take? Or perhaps those unfamiliar sights had always been there; you just never noticed them before. Such lapses can cause you to wonder if you're still fit to get behind the wheel.

Similarly, Romans 9–11 causes some people to wonder if Paul knows how to stay on track with a line of reasoning. After he exposes our sinfulness (1:18–3:20), champions the justification that comes through Christ alone (3:21–5:21), and assures us of God's faithfulness and love as we grow in Christ (6–8), we expect him to drive straight into Romans 12—and roll the rubber of our salvation onto the road of everyday life. It seems so natural, so effortless, to transition from "[nothing can] separate us from the love of God, which is in Christ Jesus our Lord" (8:39) to "Therefore I urge you, brethren, by the mercies of God, to present your bodies a living and holy sacrifice" (12:1a).

After Romans 8, however, Paul seems to veer off in another, seemingly unrelated direction—into Israel's rejection of the gospel and God's ultimate plan for the Jews. What, you might ask (and some do), does Romans 9–11 have to do with the rest of the letter? And what does it have to do with our living the Christian life?

Plenty! Romans 9–11 reminds us that God is good, sovereign, and merciful. That He does not forsake His people or forget His promises. That He can do only what is right and just. And that His Word, His grace, and His faithfulness never fall short, never fail—even in the face of human sinfulness.

So, while chapters 9–11 address the fate of nations and races, they also speak volumes to the church and to individuals about God's incomprehensible and eternal gift of righteousness to those who forsake their self-righteousness and put their trust in Christ.

And isn't that what Romans is all about? As commentator Leon Morris affirms,

> The first eleven chapters of Romans are a unity, and this is important. Paul is not here proceeding to a new and unrelated subject. These three chapters are a part of the way he makes plain how God in fact saves people.[1]

No detours here. Paul's right on track; he knows exactly where he's going. So let's get an idea of where we're going by getting a big-picture perspective—an aerial view, if you will—of Romans 9–11.

The Main Theme

If we could distill the contents of Romans 9–11 down to a single sentence, it would probably read something like this: *Paul defends God's faithfulness to Israel in light of the Jews' rejection of the gospel.* Paul has alluded to or pointed out God's special relationship with the Jews at various points in his letter (see 1:16; 3:1–8). In Romans 3:2, in fact, he began to describe the "advantages" the Jews had received from God. That list continues in 9:4. At the same time, though, he has made it clear that everyone—Jews and Gentiles alike—are under the curse of the Law and can only be saved through faith in Christ (2:17–29; 3:9–18, 21–31; chap. 4).

The nation of Israel was the apple of God's eye (Zech. 2:8); the recipient of His covenant promises. The Jews were the race from which the Messiah came. They were the guardians of the Old Testament Scriptures, which contained the gospel (see Luke 24:25–27). How is it, then, that so many Jews rejected—and continue to reject—Christ? And what effect does God's opening up His kingdom to the Gentiles have on the Jews? Has He discarded His chosen people once and for all? Does the vast number of unsaved Jews mean that God has changed His mind or somehow failed to fulfill His promises to Israel? If so, how can Christians trust what God has said about our future?

These issues center on one crucial concern, as commentator Douglas J. Moo notes: the continuity of God's plan.

---

1. Leon Morris, *The Epistle to the Romans* (1988; reprint, Grand Rapids, Mich.: William B. Eerdmans Publishing Co., 1992), p. 344.

From the beginning of the letter . . . Paul has been concerned to demonstrate that the gospel stands in continuity with the O[ld] T[estament]. He wants to make it clear that the coming of Jesus Christ and the new regime of salvation-history that he has inaugurated is no innovation in God's plan for history, but its intended culmination. However, the unbelief of the majority of Jews in Paul's day presents a potential problem for Paul's attempt to establish such continuity.[2]

In Romans 9–11, Paul sets out to address this matter and other questions his readers may be asking—with the ultimate purpose of affirming the sovereignty, goodness, and trustworthiness of God. God's plan for the Jews, Paul reassures us, is consistent with His holy character.

Other Rich Truths

In upholding God's character amid Israel's rejection, though, Paul presents a variety of other mind-stretching, heart-lifting truths. The tension of God's sovereignty and human responsibility is one of them, and James Montgomery Boice lists several more:

> (1) the historical advantages of Judaism; (2) the importance and biblical proof of election; (3) the doctrine of reprobation [God's predetermined judgment of the wicked]; (4) the justice of God in saving some and passing by others; (5) the glory of God displayed in his judgments; (6) the reason for Jewish failure to believe on Jesus of Nazareth as the Messiah; (7) the place and power of gospel preaching in God's plan; (8) the importance of Christian missions; (9) what God is doing in the present age, and why; (10) the eventual salvation of the Jews as a nation; and (11) the great and indescribable knowledge and wisdom of God that guides it all.[3]

2. Douglas J. Moo, "Romans," in the *New Bible Commentary: 21st Century Edition*, 4th ed., rev., edited by D. A. Carson, R. T. France, J. A. Motyer, and G. J. Wenham (Downers Grove, Ill.: InterVarsity Press, 1994), p. 1142.

3. James Montgomery Boice, *Romans, Volume 3: God and History (Romans 9–11)* (Grand Rapids, Mich.: Baker Books, 1993), pp. 1011–12.

We can sketch out an outline of the chapters this way:

Romans 9: God's sovereignty
Romans 10: God's justice
Romans 11: God's faithfulness

This is definitely part of the Roman road where you'll want to slow down—maybe even pull over for awhile—and take in these sweeping vistas of revelation.

The Heart of an Apostle

Let's not forget, though, where Romans 9–11 begins. With grief. Yes, grief. Paul has "great sorrow and unceasing grief" in his heart for his people (9:2). The great majority of the Jews have overlooked their own Messiah. They have mistaken their ethnicity for spiritual favor. They have zeal for keeping the Law, but not for God's gift of righteousness that comes by faith in His Son.

And if anyone knows the futility of such misguided zeal, it's Paul. In his self-righteousness, he persecuted the church—all the time thinking he was serving God. He didn't see that Jesus Christ was the long-awaited Messiah or that the gospel permeated the Old Testament Scriptures that he knew so well. He didn't see that whatever human compliance to the Law he could muster didn't take him one step closer to God. Then Christ saved him.

As a believer, Paul knew there was no injustice in God. He knew that God wasn't surprised by the Jews' rejection of Jesus. Yet his heart broke for them—as ours should too, as well as for others we know who are without Christ.

Well, that's a glimpse of what lies ahead in Romans 9–11. Before beginning the expositional study of Romans 9, pull off at the next Living Insight. There you can review and refresh yourself before journeying further.

 Living Insights

As theologically exacting as the letter to the Romans is, it doesn't obscure Paul's heart. His emotions have accompanied his theology throughout the letter. He thanks God for the Roman church's witness in the world (1:8). He waxes sarcastic to the self-righteous Jews who think they have escaped condemnation (2:17–24). He

71

angrily heaps condemnation on those who are misrepresenting his teaching (3:8). He exults as he reflects on Christ's work on behalf of sinners (5:1–11). He passionately refutes the notion that grace leads to more sin (6:1–2). He wrestles with his own depravity (7:18–19, 24) yet bursts into thanksgiving that Christ has rescued him from it (v. 25). And he grieves over those Jews who have not come to faith in Christ (9:1–3).

By his example, Paul affirms that theology isn't just supposed to fill the head; it also feeds the heart. As you reflect upon what you've studied so far in this volume of Romans, *Learning to Walk by Grace*, why not let your heart respond to some of the theology you've encountered? Just use the spaces provided after each statement to record your praise, thanks, joy, amazement, sadness . . . even any action you plan to take. Make this a time of personal devotion and application.

I'm free from sin and enslaved to Christ (6:17–18).

_____

_____

_____

_____

_____

My battle with the flesh rages on, but Christ has set me free from its domination (7:18–20, 25).

_____

_____

_____

_____

_____

Because I have placed my trust in Christ Jesus, the Law of God no longer condemns me; I am no longer the object of God's wrath (8:1).

_____

_____

_____

_____

_____

My suffering is only temporary; my hope is in the life that awaits me in glory (8:18).

_____

_____

_____

_____

_____

God knows my deepest needs, even when I can't find the words to voice them in prayer (8:26–27).

_____

_____

_____

_____

_____

My salvation, from start to finish, is secure in the hands of God (8:29–30).

_____

_____

_____

_____

_____

Nothing can separate me from God's love in Christ (8:35–39).

_____

_____

_____

_____

_____

    I have friends, family, relatives and neighbors who don't know Christ (10:1).

_____

_____

_____

_____

_____

    Next stop . . . an up-close look at Romans 9.

Chapter 10

STRAIGHT TALK ABOUT PREDESTINATION

Romans 9

 $\mathbf{D}$ on't ask, don't tell.

That's the policy many people adopt when it comes to discussing or teaching the doctrine of predestination—the belief that God predetermines whatever comes to pass, including our salvation. Some even argue that it's just better to ignore it than to get tangled up in such a heady and controversial issue.

After all, it just gets people stirred up, right? Some fume that predestination makes God unfair. Others say that it hampers personal responsibility and evangelism. Still others claim that it removes human freedom and makes us all puppets in a great cosmic show.

Whatever your position on predestination, though, one thing is for sure: If you're serious about studying or teaching the Bible (especially Paul's letter to the Romans), you can't ignore this doctrine. It's right there in plain view in Romans 9. So, rather than dismiss it, let's explore it. You just might be surprised to find that, for the Christian, predestination is one of the most comforting doctrines in all of God's Word.

Predestination: A Historical and Biblical Doctrine

Predestination isn't some wacky notion fabricated by scholars with too much time on their hands. The doctrine has been embraced throughout history by the church's most renowned theologians, pastors, and missionaries. Augustine, Martin Luther, and John Calvin all held to the doctrine of predestination. So did translators Wycliffe and Tyndale . . . and hymnwriter John Newton. William Carey, missionary to India, believed in predestination. George Whitefield and Jonathan Edwards, whose preaching launched the Great Awakening in the 1730s, taught the doctrine. We could add Charles Haddon Spurgeon, Donald Grey Barnhouse, R. C. Sproul, J. I. Packer, John Stott, and countless others.

Just because something is historical, though, doesn't automatically mean it's right. These people accepted predestination because they respected the Bible and put themselves and their theology under its holy authority. So predestination isn't just historical; it's biblical. In fact, you can't have a complete understanding of salvation without the doctrine of predestination.

Romans 9 in Context

Why does the premier passage on predestination show up here in the book of Romans? Did Paul stray from the path of practical spirituality in Romans 8 and find himself wandering aimlessly in the mysteries of God in Romans 9? Not at all. The link between Romans 9 and the rest of Romans is undeniable.

Let's remember, first of all, the theme of Romans: the righteousness of God. Paul has already made it clear that no one is righteous enough to take even one step toward God (Rom. 3:10). Righteousness is a gift that God gives to us through faith in Christ (v. 22). That means salvation isn't our work; it's God's. We have salvation, we receive the righteousness of Christ, because God chose to give it to us.

But wait. Don't we believe? Don't we put our faith in Christ? Absolutely. But conversion is not the beginning point of our salvation. Our salvation actually has its roots in the sovereign choice of God—a choice He made even "before the foundation of the world" (Eph. 1:3–6).

Commentator James Montgomery Boice points out another way that Romans 9 is a significant link in Paul's overall argument and not a diversion. He says that Romans 9–11 is

> a necessary exposition of Paul's original thesis, stated in Romans 1:16. Paul wrote there that he was "not ashamed of the gospel, because it is the power of God for the salvation of everyone who believes: first for the Jew, then for the Gentile." That is an important statement, but until this point Paul has not shown how the gospel had been presented first to Judaism. In fact, this priority appears to have been contradicted by the large-scale unbelief of this people.[1]

Also, Paul has just completed a chapter by confirming, in glowing and emotional terms, the believer's eternal security (Rom. 8:38–39).

---

1. James Montgomery Boice, *Romans, Volume 3: God and History (Romans 9–11)* (Grand Rapids, Mich.: Baker Books, 1993), pp. 1010–11.

But some of his readers must have wondered if they could truly trust in that security if

> those upon whom God had previously set his electing love, the Jewish people, have been cast off? It is all very well to affirm that nothing can separate us from the love of God in Christ. But can we believe that if many Jews, who as a people have preceded us in the long, historical, unfolding plan of salvation, have been abandoned by God and are lost?[2]

Paul obviously anticipated these questions and took the time, beginning in Romans 9, to defend the gospel—and God's trustworthiness—in light of Israel's rejection of their Messiah. And predestination, as we will see, is the crux of that defense.

Paul's Grief for the Nation of Israel

Far from being a sterile discourse on theology, Romans 9 begins with heartfelt emotion. Grief, to be exact—Paul's grief over his fellow Jews, who should embrace Christ because of their rich heritage . . . but have rejected Him instead.

> I am telling the truth in Christ, I am not lying, my conscience testifies with me in the Holy Spirit, that I have great sorrow and unceasing grief in my heart. (Rom. 9:1–2)

Paul would even trade his own salvation in order to see his "kinsmen according to the flesh," the Jews, come to faith in Christ (v. 3).[3] It would, after all, be a natural transition for them to embrace Jesus, since they have already received so many benefits that point to Him. Paul lists these benefits in verses 4 and 5:

- The adoption as sons—God's relationship with Israel as deliverer, caregiver, and provider (Exod. 4:22; Hos. 1:10; 11:1).

- The glory—God's visible presence among the Israelites, which shone from Sinai and filled the tabernacle and temple (Exod. 13:21–22; 24:15–17; 40:34–35; 1 Kings 8:11).

2. Boice, *Romans, Volume 3*, p. 1011.

3. Paul knew, of course, that trading his own salvation for that of the Jews wouldn't be possible. But his statement demonstrates the love he has for his fellow Jews and his desire to see them come to faith in Christ.

- The covenants—the covenant given to Abraham and renewed with Isaac and Jacob, along with the covenants made with Moses and David, and the new covenant (Gen. 15:18–21; 17:4–21; 26:3–5; 28:13–15; 35:9–12; Exod. 19–24; Deut. 29:9–15; 2 Sam. 7:16; Jer. 31:33).

- The giving of the Law—God's holy standards, written by His own finger at Sinai (Exod. 20:1–17; Lev. 18–19; the book of Deuteronomy).

- The temple service—the Israelites' whole system of worship, including the tabernacle and, later, the temple, the priesthood, and the sacrifices (Exod. 25–31; 35–40; the book of Leviticus).

- The promises—particularly the promises of the coming Messiah (Gen. 3:15; Pss. 32; 110; Isa. 53; and myriad other Old Testament passages).

- The fathers—the patriarchs: Abraham, Isaac, Jacob, and Jacob's twelve sons. From these the human ancestry of Christ can be traced (see genealogy in Matt. 1:1–17).

- Jesus Christ, who was Himself a Jew, and whom all the previous benefits foreshadow.

With all these benefits, it seems unthinkable that a Jew would reject Jesus Christ. But the majority had. And for some skeptics, that called into question the validity of God's promises to bless Israel. So Paul now sets out to show that Israel's rejection of their Messiah neither impugns God's character nor invalidates His plan.

Salvation Begins with Predestination

> But it is not as though the word of God has failed. For they are not all Israel who are descended from Israel; nor are they all children because they are Abraham's descendants, but: "through Isaac your descendants will be named." That is, it is not the children of the flesh who are children of God, but the children of the promise are regarded as descendants. For this is the word of promise: "At this time I will come, and Sarah shall have a son." (Rom. 9:6–9)

Isaac, not Ishmael, was the child promised to Abraham (see Gen. 17:15–22). He represents God's predetermined plan to bless the Jews and call them to Himself. This redemptive plan has not been thwarted by Israel's rejection of Jesus as their Messiah. No, God's plan will still be worked out.

After the church is raptured in the end times, God's gaze will return to Israel, and many Jews will place their trust in Jesus Christ. These believing Jews—more than merely the physical descendants of Abraham—will see the fulfillment of many of God's promises to His people recorded in the Old Testament. *The New Scofield Reference Bible* elaborates:

> The distinction is between Israel after the flesh, the mere natural posterity of Abraham, and Israelites who through faith are also Abraham's spiritual children. Gentiles who believe are also of Abraham's spiritual seed; but here the apostle is not considering them but only the two kinds of Israelites—the natural and the spiritual Israel.[4]

So, even though Israel as a whole currently rejects their Messiah, many of them will one day come to faith in Jesus, thus fulfilling God's promises to redeem the Jews to Himself. Why will many of them embrace Christ while others will reject Him? Because of God's predetermined choice, as Paul indicates with the example of God's choosing Jacob over Esau (Rom. 9:10–13). Before either of these brothers had drawn his first breath or had a chance to do anything good or bad, God had already determined to elect Jacob and reject Esau—to direct salvation history through Jacob's line, not Esau's.

Does Predestination Make God Unjust?

"How unfair!" we want to cry in our finiteness. For God to choose some and reject others seems so arbitrary. To this objection Paul responds,

> What shall we say then? There is no injustice with God, is there? May it never be! For He says to Moses, "I will have mercy on whom I will have mercy, and I will have compassion on whom I have compassion." So then it does not depend on the man

---

4. *The New Scofield Reference Bible*, ed. C. I. Scofield (New York, N.Y.: Oxford University Press, 1967), footnote on p. 1223.

who wills or the man who runs, but on God who has mercy. (vv. 14–16)

Salvation is God's work . . . and God's work alone. We can't do enough good deeds, make enough sound decisions, or muster enough determination to earn eternal life. Our holy and loving God, for reasons known only to Him, has chosen to select some sinners out of the mass of humanity, save them from His judgment, and bless them with eternal life. So predestination not only upholds God's justice and goodness, but it magnifies His mercy and love.

What about those, though, whom God doesn't choose for salvation? Those whom He leaves in their sin? What attributes of God do they magnify?

> For the Scripture says to Pharaoh, "For this very purpose I raised you up, to demonstrate My power in you, and that My name might be proclaimed throughout the whole earth." So then He has mercy on whom He desires, and He hardens whom He desires. (vv. 17–18)

The demonstration of God's power and justice. The advancement of His great Name. That was God's predetermined purpose for Pharaoh. But wait. Does that mean God forced Pharaoh, and everyone else who opposes Him, to sin? Or that He capriciously created Pharaoh for no other reason than to destroy him? Again, the underlying question relates to God's character. Commentator Leon Morris helps us understand this idea of God's "hardening" people.

> Let us notice first that neither here nor anywhere else is God said to harden anyone who had not first hardened himself. We must bear in mind that, while God is repeatedly said to have hardened Pharaoh (Exod. 9:12; 10:1, 20, 27; 11:10; 14:8; there are also prophecies that he will do this [Exod. 4:21; 7:3]), it is also true that Pharaoh is repeatedly said to have hardened himself (Exod. 7:13, 14, 22; 8:15, 19, 32; 9:7, 34, 35 . . . cf. also Exod. 13:15). God's hardening follows on what Pharaoh himself did. His hardening always presupposes sin and is always part of the punishment of sin. God could kill the sinner immediately when he sinned, but he usually does not. But he shuts him up to the effect of his sin, so

that the person who hardens himself is condemned to live as a hardened person. God does not harden people who do not go astray first (cf. Jas. 1:13).[5]

But can Pharaoh or anyone else be held responsible for their sin if judgment was somehow part of God's plan from the beginning? Doesn't predestination let sinners off the hook as far as their accountability for their sins and the consequences of their unbelief? Good questions . . . and Paul answers them next.

He Is the Potter; We Are the Clay

You will say to me then, "Why does He still find fault? For who resists His will?" On the contrary, who are you, O man, who answers back to God? The thing molded will not say to the molder, "Why did you make me like this," will it? Or does the potter have a right over the clay, to make from the same lump one vessel for honorable use and another for common use? (Rom. 9:19–21)

Paul isn't condemning the asking of sincere, searching questions. Rather, he's dealing with a spirit of rebellion—those who call into question God's sovereign right to do as He wishes with His creatures. That's as foolish as clay asking the potter to explain himself.[6] Paul's answer isn't a cop-out. It's a reminder that God works according to His own perfect counsel and wisdom, even though we may not understand all His reasons.

Let's not, however, confuse God's mystery with capriciousness or sinful secrecy. He is and does only good. And, though He predestines, He doesn't *make* anyone sin. People sin because they want to.

What if God, although willing to demonstrate His wrath and to make His power known, endured with much patience vessels of wrath prepared for destruction? And He did so to make known the riches of His glory upon vessels of mercy, which He prepared beforehand for glory. (vv. 22–23)

5. Leon Morris, *The Epistle to the Romans* (1988; reprint, Grand Rapids, Mich.: William B. Eerdmans Publishing Co., 1992), p. 361.

6. In the image of the potter and the clay, Paul isn't dealing so much with God's creating humanity as he is with God's divine prerogative to do as He wishes with sinful humanity.

God is good. He is just. He is holy. He is all-wise. He is rich in mercy. His perfect character makes it impossible for Him to do anything other than that which is right. Even the unbelievers He judges, He "endures with much patience" before judging (v. 22). Why? So that against the ultimate judgment of those who reject Him, the "riches of His glory upon vessels of mercy" will shine forth (v. 23). God's judgment, in other words, provides the dark backdrop for the glorious, glittering jewel of God's mercy. When believers ponder the judgment we as sinners deserve, the mercy God has lavished on us in Christ is all the brighter.

Wanting to shift his readers' focus from questioning God's character to celebrating His mercy, Paul calls them to consider how God has plucked all believers, Jews and Gentiles alike, off the road to certain judgment and lavished His mercy on them (vv. 24–29). We who were once not His people are now His people (v. 25a). His beloved (v. 25b). His children (v. 26b). And in His faithful mercy, He holds onto the remnant of Israel (v. 27). We all are the clay that the merciful hand of the Potter has molded for "honorable" use.

Conclusion

The final four verses of chapter 9 confirm that the Jews' rejection of their Messiah does not impugn the character of God. He is still gathering a people to Himself—by faith, not by law-keeping (vv. 30–31). Those who try to become righteous by keeping the Law will stumble over Him (vv. 32–33a). Those who believe in Him by faith "will not be disappointed" (v. 33b). John Stott writes that

> everybody has to decide how to relate to this rock [Christ] which God has laid down. There are only two possibilities. One is to put our trust in him, to take him as the foundation of our lives and build on him. The other is to bark our shins against him, and so to stumble and fall.[7]

We can't tell by looking whom God has chosen for salvation and whom He has chosen for judgment. That is why we have the gospel. As we extend the offer of salvation, His elect will believe. His mercy will be exalted. And His promises to gather a people to Himself will be fulfilled.

7. John Stott, *Romans: God's Good News for the World* (Downers Grove, Ill.: InterVarsity Press, 1994), p. 277.

Living Insights

That's a lot to absorb in one sitting, isn't it? Predestination takes some time to ponder. And the longer we do, the more God's grace and mercy come to light. "How can a loving God send people to hell?" just doesn't seem to be the most important question anymore. The more staggering question is, "How can a holy and righteous God who cannot look upon sin allow any of sinful humanity to enjoy the blessing of eternal life?"

We can only probe so far into the mysteries of God. He simply hasn't revealed everything about Himself to us. But we know that a big part of the answer is love. Predestination means that God loved us before we loved Him. Before we knew Him. Before creation. Even before time. If we have placed our trust in Christ, we have been loved with a divine love, an eternal love. A love that transcends everything temporal—circumstances, feelings, doubts . . . death.

The theology of Romans 9 explains Paul's exultation in Romans 8. Nothing can separate us from the love of God, because God's choice to love us and redeem us in Christ is an everlasting choice. His love for us began in eternity past. It will carry us through this life. And it will sustain us forever.

Predestination. It's more than theological information. It's a love letter from God to us, telling us that He has loved us (and will love us) forever.

Chapter 11

STRAIGHT TALK ABOUT RESPONSIBILITY

Romans 10

In the previous chapter, we explored the relationship between predestination and national Israel's unbelief. Paul explained that the nation as a whole did not embrace Christ because God had predestined only a remnant to believe.

We also learned, though, that predestination doesn't let those who reject Christ off the hook. They're still responsible for their actions. God hardened Pharaoh (Rom. 9:17–18), but Pharaoh's heart—just like every sinful human heart—was already hard toward God.

In Romans 10, Paul moves from the divine side of unbelief to the human side, as he continues to address the phenomenon of Israel's rejection of the gospel. The majority of Israel, we will find, is lost because they have chosen to pursue their own righteousness rather than trust in the righteousness of Christ.

People sin because they want to, not because God makes them. They refuse to heed the message of Christ because it's in their sin nature to do so. So God, even though He predestines, rightly holds the unregenerate responsible for their rebellion against Him.

Predestination, however, doesn't let *believers* off the hook either. We also have a responsibility—to herald the gospel of grace. God has chosen a people for Himself. But He has also arranged that they come to faith through hearing the gospel. So believers must proclaim Christ as the way of salvation—whether people embrace or discard that message. For how can anyone "believe in Him whom they have not heard" (10:14)?

Let's hear what Paul has to say, then, about the responsibility of those who reject Christ . . . and of those who love Him.

Paul's Desire for Israel's Salvation

As he did in Romans 9, Paul expresses his heartfelt desire for Israel's salvation (10:1). They have great zeal for God, but that very zeal keeps them from Christ. It is "not in accordance with knowledge" (v. 2b). Rather, it's based on their desire to become righteous on their own, which is really just a passionate self-righteousness, rather than by trusting in the righteousness God grants in Christ (v. 3; see also 9:30–33).

Jesus Christ, though, is "the end of the law for righteousness to everyone who believes" (10:4). That is, He brings an end to our futile attempts to become righteous through law-keeping. Sometimes those who seem the most religious, the most passionate about keeping all the rules, need the gospel the most—and often reject it most fiercely.

The Unbeliever's Responsibility: Responding to Christ

One might be tempted to argue that the Old Testament and its Law are all the Jews had. Yet it's not as though the Old Testament had nothing to teach them about Christ—He's everywhere in it (see, for example, Gen. 3:15 and Isa. 53; see also Luke 24:25–27; John 5:39; Rom. 1:2).

And Christ's way of righteousness isn't based on law-keeping. His is a "righteousness based on faith." Referring to Deuteronomy 30, Paul quotes Moses as he explains this point.

> For Moses writes that the man who practices the righteousness which is based on law shall live by that righteousness. But the righteousness based on faith speaks as follows: "Do not say in your heart, 'Who will ascend into heaven?' (that is, to bring Christ down), or 'Who will descend into the abyss?' (that is, to bring Christ up from the dead)." But what does it say? "The word is near you, in your mouth and in your heart"—that is, the word of faith which we are preaching. (Rom. 10:5–8)

Neither the Jews nor anyone else can "ascend into heaven" or "descend into the abyss." In other words, no one but Christ could make the Incarnation and Resurrection happen, so no one can construct salvation from their own means, apart from Christ. The Jews, however, did not recognize the One who accomplished these events on their behalf.

Paul's point in drawing on Deuteronomy 30 and applying that passage to Christ seems to be to convince the Jews that righteousness is something done for us, not something we do for ourselves. It comes through faith in Jesus Christ, God in the flesh, who lived a perfect life under the Law, then died and rose again for our salvation. Salvation has come; it is within reach. It is as close as a decision of the heart and a declaration of the mouth (vv. 8–10).

And He is accessible to *anyone* who will believe—Jews and Gentiles alike. The offer of salvation is a universal offer.

> For the Scripture says, "Whoever believes in Him will not be disappointed." For there is no distinction between Jew and Greek; for the same Lord is Lord of all, abounding in riches for all who call on Him; for "Whoever will call on the name of the Lord will be saved." (vv. 11–13)

Paul once again draws on the Old Testament, probably for two reasons. One, to reemphasize that salvation by faith has always been God's plan. It is nothing new. It's in the Old Testament, so the Jews, of all people, should have grasped it. A second reason, though, might be that Paul wanted to stress the opening up of the kingdom of God to all people. A message confined primarily to national Israel in the Old Testament is now spread abroad to all people in the church age. And that's where the personal responsibility of believers comes in today.

The Believer's Responsibility: Proclaiming Christ

> How then will they call on Him in whom they have not believed? How will they believe in Him whom they have not heard? And how will they hear without a preacher? How will they preach unless they are sent? (vv. 14–15a)

Paul shifts his emphasis now from the acceptance or rejection of the message to its delivery. He has already said that whoever calls "on the name of the Lord will be saved" (v. 13). But before people can call on the Lord and place their trust in Christ, they must believe the truth of the gospel. They must recognize that Jesus Christ is the only One who can save them from sin.

To believe the gospel, however, one must hear it. And for it to be heard, it must be heralded. And such heralds must be sent for the purpose of declaring the gospel. Commentator John Murray unfolds the logical progression of these two verses for us.

> The main point is that the saving relation to Christ involved in calling upon his name is not something

that can occur in a vacuum; it occurs only in a context created by proclamation of the gospel on the part of those commissioned to proclaim it. The sequence is therefore: authorized messengers, proclamation, hearing, faith [or belief], calling on the Lord's name.[1]

This progression charges the church to take up the task of evangelism deliberately and passionately. To yearn for the salvation of the lost. To equip our flocks for evangelism—helping them to not only know the truth but to communicate it. To train and commission people with the specific task of preaching the gospel—pastors, missionaries, evangelists. To send them out and support them in their work.

This is the process God has ordained for scattering the seed of His gospel. And what a privilege it is for us to be involved in that plan. Paul says of those who deliver the message of salvation: "How beautiful are the feet of those who bring good news of good things" (v. 15b). These words, originally recorded by Isaiah, referred to the good news given to the Jews who would be exiled to Babylon that their captivity would be over and they would return to their own land (Isa. 52:7).

How much more joyous is the news that we bring to the lost: that Jesus Christ forgives sins and gives eternal life to all who will turn to Him!

Not All Who Hear Will Respond

Not everyone, however, welcomes this wonderful message—as confirmed by Israel's unbelief. They "did not all heed the good news," even though they most certainly heard it (Rom. 10:16–18). So they can't use the excuse that the gospel never reached them. Did they just lack understanding, then? Did they not "know" (v. 19a)? Paul again quotes from Deuteronomy:

> "I will make you jealous by that which is not a
> nation,
> By a nation without understanding will I anger you."
> (v. 19b; see Deut. 32:21)

---

1. John Murray, *The Epistle to the Romans* (Grand Rapids, Mich.: William B. Eerdmans Publishing Co., 1965), vol. 2, p. 58.

This quote makes it clear that the people "without understanding" were the Gentiles, not the Jews. The Jews, we already know, possessed all the benefits that pointed to Christ (Rom. 9:4–5; see also 3:1–2). Not understanding, not knowing, then, is also no excuse. Ironically, it was the Gentiles who were turning to Christ when Israel was rejecting their own Messiah. As Paul quotes Isaiah again,

> "I was found by those who did not seek Me,
> I became manifest to those who did not ask for Me."
> (Rom. 10:20; see Isa. 65:1)

So what is the reason for Israel's unbelief? In a word: *stubbornness*.

> But as for Israel He says, "All the day long I have stretched out My hands to a disobedient and obstinate people." (Rom. 10:21)

What a picture! God's holding out His hands

> indicates a gesture of dual purpose: one of welcome and one of giving. But God's welcome was spurned and his gifts were rejected.
>
> The disobedience of *Israel* was judged by God's welcome to the Gentiles (even though that was in his plan all along). But he will still accept his chosen people if they will only return to him. He remains faithful to his promises to his people, even though they have been unfaithful to him. God still holds out his hands.[2]

More specifically, as James Montgomery Boice writes, it is Christ's hand we must take to be saved.

> It is a wounded hand that holds out salvation to you and invites you to come. Reach out and touch that hand. Then allow it to enfold you in an embrace that nothing on earth or in heaven will ever diminish or disturb.[3]

2. Bruce B. Barton, David R. Veerman, and Neil Wilson, *Romans*, Life Application Bible Commentary Series (Wheaton, Ill.: Tyndale House Publishers, 1992), p. 205.

3. James Montgomery Boice, *Romans, Volume 3: God and History (Romans 9–11)* (Grand Rapids, Mich.: Baker Books, 1993), p. 1284.

If you do not yet know Christ, fulfill your responsibility—reach out and take His nail-scarred hand and be saved. If you do know Him, embrace the responsibility of holding out His invitation to others. And you will know the joy of bringing "good news of good things" (v. 15).

 ## *Living Insights*

Some people are just gifted, literally, when it comes to evangelism (see Eph. 4:11). Those who possess that spiritual gift seem to blend the gospel into everyday discussion as effortlessly as a soft breeze caresses its way through a grove of trees.

Not everyone, though, is gifted in evangelism. Not everyone is called to be a dynamic preacher. But we can all talk about our faith at some level, can't we? And we can all improve both our knowledge of truth and the way we communicate it.

Without being too hard on yourself, why not do a little reflecting about how proactive you are these days when it comes to sharing your faith.

First, is there someone in your regular sphere of family, work, or social life whom you feel you know well enough to engage in a discussion about Christianity? Is there someone with whom you spend a lot of time who hasn't heard about Christ from you yet? What names come to mind?

_____

_____

_____

If you've got someone in mind, what interests does this person have that might make a good springboard into a discussion about Christ?

_____

_____

_____

How can you blend thought-provoking questions, Scripture passages, Christian perspectives on current events, into a discussion with this person that might pique his or her interest?

_____

_____

_____

What tough questions can you anticipate from this person that you could do some thinking about ahead of time?

_____

_____

_____

What reading material, tapes, or other resources can you give this person to keep the dialogue going over time?

_____

_____

_____

Since, hopefully, you know by this point in our study of Romans that salvation is God's work and not ours, how does that relieve the pressure for you when sharing the truth about Jesus?

_____

_____

_____

You don't need to feel pressured to "close the sale" the first time you bring up the topic or "get someone saved" in order to improve your standing with God. Our responsibility is to get the truth out there. Those whom God has elected will respond in faith through the working of the Holy Spirit.

So study the Scriptures. Read widely. Be aware of what's happening in the world, and look at those events through the lens of a Christian worldview. Think about the big questions of life people ask—but don't think you have to have all the answers. Be natural. Be attentive. And there's no reason why you can't discuss your faith clearly and competently. May God bless you as you bring "good news of good things" to those around you.

Chapter 12

THE JEW:
CAST OFF OR SET ASIDE?

Romans 11:1–14

As we enter Romans 11, Paul is wrapping up his discussion of God's dealings with Israel.

In Romans 9, he emphasized that the Jews who embraced Christ did so because they were predestined to believe, while the others had not been chosen by God. In chapter 10, however, Paul made it clear that the Jews who rejected their Messiah did so of their own choice—their coldness toward Christ was their fault, not God's.

Has God, then, cast off the nation of Israel for good? Are they no longer part of His plan? These are the questions Paul now sets out to answer in Romans 11.

The Question: Has God Rejected His People?

Paul begins by asking the very question he anticipates his readers will ask.

> I say then, God has not rejected His people, has He? (Rom. 11:1a)

Surely even God has a limit to His patience. Since the Jews had rejected their Messiah, wouldn't He now reject them as well? "May it never be!" is Paul's emphatically negative reply (v. 1b).

The Evidence

How can Paul be so sure that God would not abandon His people? He presents four pieces of evidence to support his certainty of God's faithfulness: his own conversion, God's foreknowledge of His people, the existence of a believing remnant, and Israel's temporary hardening.

Paul, an Israelite

Paul is living proof that Jews can come to faith in Christ.

> For I too am an Israelite, a descendant of Abraham,
> of the tribe of Benjamin. (v. 1b)

At one time, Paul hated Christ and persecuted His church. Then Jesus saved him—He changed his heart and turned him into His most fervent spokesman. Obviously, if God were finished with the Jews, He wouldn't have used Paul—or for that matter, Peter, James, John, or any of the other apostles—to build His kingdom, for they were all Jews.

Those Whom God Foreknew

God has not rejected His people whom He foreknew. (v. 2a)

Foreknowledge and rejection are incompatible. How could God love and choose a people for Himself, then later reject them? He couldn't, because He never goes back on His word.

Paul isn't saying here, of course, that God chose all Jews to be saved. That would contradict his whole line of argument. Remember, he has been explaining for two chapters why not all Jews have come to Christ. Rather, Paul is talking about God's foreknowing national Israel as His covenant people—choosing them to be "the people through whom all other nations of the world could know him."[1] That means there is still a place in His plan for national Israel.

The Existence of a Remnant

Another piece of evidence to show that God has not turned His back on the Jews is the existence of a believing remnant. Even in times of great apostasy, God has reserved for Himself a group of people who belong to Him by faith. Paul cites Elijah's day as an example.

> Or do you not know what the Scriptures say in the passage about Elijah, how he pleads with God against Israel? "Lord, they have killed Your prophets, they have torn down Your altars, and I alone am left, and they are seeking my life." But what is the divine response to him? "I have kept for Myself seven thousand men who have not bowed the knee to Baal." In the same way then, there has also come to be at the present time a remnant according to God's

1. Bruce B. Barton, David R. Veerman, and Neil Wilson, *Romans*, Life Application Bible Commentary Series (Wheaton, Ill.: Tyndale House Publishers, 1992), p. 208.

gracious choice. But if it is by grace, it is no longer on the basis of works, otherwise grace is no longer grace. (vv. 2b–6)

After calling down the fire of God on Mount Carmel and getting rid of the prophets of Baal (1 Kings 18:36–40), Elijah's life was in danger. The wicked Jezebel, wife of cowardly King Ahab, had vowed to track down the prophet and kill him (19:2). This threat, as well as Elijah's assumption that there were no more followers of the true God left in Israel, made him feel terribly alone and outnumbered— like the only true believer in all of Israel.

God, however, reminded the prophet that he was not alone in his devotion to the Lord. And neither was Paul; God was calling some of the apostle's fellow Jews to Himself. Not those who persisted in trying to work their way to God, but those who rested by faith in God's merciful grace.

And we are not alone either. Even when it looks as though the whole world has forgotten God, remember . . . there is a remnant. And upon that remnant of believers, chosen by God's grace alone, God is lavishing His blessings. Through them, He is working out His plan of salvation.

The Spiritual Hardening of Israel

You might be surprised to find, though, that God's plan includes national Israel's hardness toward Jesus.

> What then? What Israel is seeking, it has not
> obtained, but those who were chosen obtained it,
> and the rest were hardened; just as it is written,
> "God gave them a spirit of stupor,
> Eyes to see not and ears to hear not,
> Down to this very day."
> And David says,
> "Let their table become a snare and a trap,
> And a stumbling block and a retribution
>   to them.
> Let their eyes be darkened to see not,
> And bend their backs forever." (Rom. 11:7–10)

Once again Paul draws on the Old Testament to further his argument—this time Deuteronomy 29:4, Isaiah 29:10, and Psalm 69:22–23. The first two passages describe Israel's lack of belief and understanding, a "spiritual stupor" producing

> a kind of numbness that results in blindness . . .
> and deafness. . . . When people repeatedly refuse
> to listen to God's Good News, they eventually will
> be unable to hear and understand it.[2]

Psalm 69 is David's plea for God to judge the wicked who are persecuting him. It's also a messianic psalm foreshadowing the suffering of Jesus. Commentator John A. Witmer sheds some light on Paul's use of two of its verses.

> The very things which should have been the source
> of nourishment and blessing to Israel (*table* means
> their blessings from the hand of God, which should
> have led them to Christ; cf. Gal. 3:24) became the
> occasion for their rejection of God (*a snare and a
> trap, a stumbling block;* cf. Rom. 9:32–33) and God's
> judgment (*retribution*) on them. Because they refused
> to receive God's truth (cf. Isa. 6:9–10; John 5:40)
> *their backs* will be bent under the weight of guilt and
> punishment *forever.*[3]

So, God has left those Jews who have rejected the Messiah to their own devices. He has judged them by turning them over to their unbelief. That doesn't mean all Jews will perish in their sins, though. Some will come to faith in Christ through the faith of the Gentiles.

Blessings for Jews and Gentiles

> I say then, they did not stumble so as to fall, did
> they? May it never be! But by their transgression
> salvation has come to the Gentiles, to make them
> jealous. Now if their transgression is riches for the
> world and their failure is riches for the Gentiles, how
> much more will their fulfillment be! (Rom. 11:11–12)

Israel has stumbled but not fallen beyond hope. God has not completely discarded them. In fact, their rejection of Jesus is part

---

2. Barton, Veerman, and Wilson, *Romans*, p. 211.

3. John A. Witmer, "Romans," in *The Bible Knowledge Commentary*, New Testament edition, ed. John F. Walvoord and Roy B. Zuck (Colorado Springs, Colo.: Chariot Victor Publishing, 1983), p. 483.

of God's plan to eventually bring many Jews to faith. In the mean-time, their "transgression," their unbelief, has caused the gospel to be taken to the Gentiles.

When Jesus came, He came to the lost sheep of Israel. But all during His ministry, Gentiles were coming to faith in Him, while the Jewish religious leaders refused to believe He was the Son of God. Paul, too, went first to the Jews. But their hardness of heart caused him to focus his ministry on the Gentiles, where he found soil plowed and ready to receive the seed of the gospel.

So you see, reaching the Gentiles through the Jews' unbelief was part of God's plan all along. But the blessing doesn't stop with the Gentiles. God designed their belief, in turn, to "make [the Jews] jealous." And if the Gentiles' belief because of the Jews' rejection is a blessing, how much more of a blessing will Israel's eventual belief be!

God has not rejected His people. And this is a great encour-agement to Paul, who sees his mission to the Gentiles as a double blessing—immediate salvation of the Gentiles and eventual salva-tion of the Jews.

> But I am speaking to you who are Gentiles. Inasmuch
> then as I am an apostle of Gentiles, I magnify my
> ministry, if somehow I might move to jealousy my
> fellow countrymen and save some of them. (vv. 13–14)

What a heart the apostle Paul had for the lost! May we be as grieved over those we know who do not know the Savior. And may we be as eager to tell them about the forgiveness, love, and life He offers.

 ## Living Insights

I'm assuming most of the people reading this study guide are non-Jews. And as non-Jews, we're faced with a question posed by Paul's words in Romans 11:1–14. How are we to view non-believing Jews in our day and age?

Let's run through some options. We could view them as com-pletely beyond the reach of Jesus Christ. Hopeless. Not worth our time. Completely closed to the gospel. But that doesn't fit with Paul's assurance that God hasn't written off all the Jews, does it? And it certainly doesn't reflect the hope of salvation Paul held for his people.

Or we could pridefully look down on them, gloating over the fact that we possess the treasure they discarded. Yet how foolish we would be to boast in our salvation, which has come by God's grace alone. We have nothing to boast in, except God and His mercy (Rom. 3:27; 4:2; 9:15–17; 11:6).

We could go to the other extreme and view our Jewish friends as fellow believers. We could forget our doctrinal differences and declare, "Hey, we pretty much believe the same thing, don't we? I mean, after all, Jesus was a Jew. And we both believe in God, right?"

And that wouldn't be right, either. After all, Jesus said that He was the only way to the Father. It is through Him and Him alone that we receive forgiveness of sins and eternal life. Jesus is the second Person of the Trinity. And when Jews deny Jesus' deity, they deny the triunity of God.

So, what do we do? To begin with, we should honestly acknowledge that the roots of our faith go deep into Judaism (see 3:1–2; 9:4–5). The Law, the sacrificial system, the covenants—all these and more point to Jesus Christ. We should be thankful for such a rich heritage.

Second, if our sphere of daily life includes any Jews, we should try to engage them in discussion about the identity of their messiah. If they're open to listening, we have a great opportunity to show them Jesus in their own Scriptures—the Old Testament. New Testament epistles, such as Romans and Hebrews, extensively quote the Old Testament and are a great place to start. From such books, we can show how Jesus Christ was presented in many types in the Old Testament and was indeed their promised Messiah.

Do you know any Jewish people? What are their names?

_____

_____

How can you best approach these people? How will you start the discussion? What are some good opening questions you can ask?

_____

_____

_____

_____

What kind of thought-provoking materials can you leave with them?

_____

_____

_____

Now, will you commit to pray for them?

_____

Just remember, no nationality has exclusive claim to Jesus Christ. We are saved *by faith*, not by bloodline or social status or anything else.

> There is neither Jew nor Greek, there is neither slave nor free man, there is neither male nor female; for you are all one in Christ Jesus. And if you belong to Christ, then you are Abraham's descendants, heirs according to promise. (Gal. 3:28–29)

Chapter 13

HORTICULTURAL ETHICS

Romans 11:15–29

As we learned in the previous chapter, God's plan of the ages still reserves a place for Jews as individuals and as a nation. Paul himself was proof that God has not rejected the Jews individually. And God hasn't rejected the Jews as a nation either, even though He has set them aside for awhile because of their unbelief.

The Gentiles have actually benefited from the Jews' disobedience, for through Israel's sin God has brought salvation to the world. Yet God has not closed the book on the Jews. In the future, He will write the final chapter of the Hebrew saga when He restores Israel to their original place of favor, just as He promised in the Old Testament. God always keeps His promises.

The *hows* and *whys* of His plan, we may never fully comprehend. In many ways, God's plan is beyond understanding—as an old preacher once warned, it's unwise to try to "fathom the unfathomable or unscrew the inscrutable." However, some of the practical implications of God's dealings with the nations are within our reach. One has to do with how Jews and Gentiles should get along. In this section of Romans 11, Paul draws powerful word pictures to help us learn how to relate to one another in humility and grace.

Two Clarifying Metaphors

Paul offers two word pictures—one taken from the kitchen and the other from the garden.

The Lump of Dough

The first word picture compares the Jewish nation to a lump of dough.

> For if [the Jews'] rejection is the reconciliation of the world, what will their acceptance be but life from the dead? If the first piece of dough is holy, the lump is also. (Rom. 11:15–16a)

Paul's argument is this: If Israel's rejecting the Messiah brought salvation to the world, certainly their accepting Him will produce at least an equal blessing for the Jews. It's important for Paul's

Roman Gentile readers to understand that the Jews may be set *aside*, but they are still set *apart* as God's covenant people.

To illustrate Israel's special place in God's program, Paul refers to the ancient Jewish practice of consecrating the first piece of dough made from the grain of the new harvest (see Num. 15:20–21). John A. Witmer explains that "since it is set apart to the Lord first, it sanctifies the whole harvest."[1] The parallel, then, is that the patriarchs—Abraham, Isaac, and Jacob—consecrated the generations of Jews to follow.

The Root and Branches

Paul's second illustration drives the point home:

> And if the root is holy, the branches are too. (v. 16b)

Just as life-giving sap flows from the root of a tree through the trunk into the branches, the covenant blessing in Abraham (the root of Israel) courses through each limb of the Jewish nation. Nothing—not even the terrible sin of rejecting the Messiah—can stop up the flow and cause God to revoke His covenant. And yet, because of their transgression, the Jews must endure God's hand of judgment. As a result, writes Bible scholar John Stott, the Jews "are objects of God's love and wrath simultaneously."[2]

This begs the question: How should Paul's Roman readers relate to the Jews—as objects of God's love or as objects of His wrath? As brothers or enemies?

Words of Warning

The Gentile Christians in Rome may have been tempted to brush off the Jews with an air of anti-Semitic superiority. So Paul continues his analogy of the root and branches with a word of caution against arrogance.

> But if some of the branches were broken off, and
> you, being a wild olive, were grafted in among them
> and became partaker with them of the rich root of

---

1. John A. Witmer, "Romans," in *The Bible Knowledge Commentary*, New Testament edition, ed. John F. Walvoord and Roy B. Zuck (Colorado Springs, Colo.: Chariot Victor Publishing, 1983), p. 484.

2. John Stott, *Romans: God's Good News for the World* (Downers Grove, Ill.: InterVarsity Press, 1994), p. 306.

the olive tree, do not be arrogant toward the branches; but if you are arrogant, remember that it is not you who supports the root, but the root supports you. You will say then, "Branches were broken off so that I might be grafted in." Quite right, they were broken off for their unbelief, but you stand by your faith. Do not be conceited, but fear; for if God did not spare the natural branches, He will not spare you, either. (vv. 17–21)

Paul's warning here reminds us of his caution to the Corinthians: "Therefore let him who thinks he stands take heed that he does not fall" (1 Cor. 10:12). The Gentiles took the place of the Jews, not because they were worthier, but because of God's grace alone. Before Christ, Gentiles were "separate . . . excluded . . . strangers to the covenants of promise, having no hope and without God in the world" (Eph. 2:12). As pagan idolaters, they were like the wild olive tree—the hillside scrub of Palestine. Bitter, shriveled fruit hung from their limbs, making them unfit for God's orchard. It is only by grace that they have been grafted into God's succulent tree of life.[3]

If the Gentiles are not careful, though, they might repeat the Jews' mistake and receive a similar fate:

> Behold then the kindness and severity of God; to those who fell, severity, but to you, God's kindness, if you continue in His kindness; otherwise you also will be cut off. (Rom. 11:22)

Cut off? Do these verses mean that if we fall into sin, we will lose our salvation?

Let's proceed with caution here. If the olive tree symbolizes salvation or the church, as some Bible scholars say, then "cut off" might mean that we can lose our salvation. But that is not what we believe the olive tree represents. What does it represent, then? Bible scholar Alva McClain offers an answer.

> [The olive tree] represents the place of favor or privilege. Abraham is the root, for "salvation is of the

---

3. Because the branch contains the fruit-bearing capacity, a gardener normally grafts an orchard-quality branch to a wild stock, never the opposite. By reversing the usual procedure, Paul shows us that, in God's orchard, the true value is in the root, not the branch, and even a worthless branch can produce good fruit when the divine life flows through it.

Jews" (Jn 4:22). God first brought into favor the Jew, then He cast him out of favor and put in the Gentile. It does not save anyone to be in this olive tree.[4]

In the Old Testament, Israel claimed "most favored nation" status with God because of the Abrahamic covenant. Yet that status didn't mean each individual Jew was saved. Salvation was—and still is—a matter of personal faith. By the same token, although the Gentiles now are included in God's blessing to Abraham, they are not saved on those grounds alone. Their new position of favor *makes it possible* for them to be saved, but it doesn't save them. So "cut off" means losing the position of favor, not losing salvation.

What would happen if the Jews as a nation became receptive to Jesus as their Messiah? Would God restore them to their former glory? Certainly!

> And they also, if they do not continue in their unbelief, will be grafted in, for God is able to graft them in again. For if you were cut off from what is by nature a wild olive tree, and were grafted contrary to nature into a cultivated olive tree, how much more will these who are the natural branches be grafted into their own olive tree? (vv. 23–24)

God's Plan for the Future

The regrafting of the Jews turns Paul's thoughts to the future . . . and a divine mystery:

> For I do not want you, brethren, to be uninformed of this mystery—so that you will not be wise in your own estimation—that a partial hardening has happened to Israel until the fullness of the Gentiles has come in; and so all Israel will be saved; just as it is written,
> "The Deliverer will come from Zion,
> He will remove ungodliness from Jacob."
> "This is My covenant with them,
> When I take away their sins." (vv. 25–27)

---

4. Alva J. McClain, *Romans: The Gospel of God's Grace* (The Lectures of Alva J. McClain), comp. and ed. Herman A. Hoyt (Chicago, Ill.: Moody Press, 1973), p. 201.

By *mystery*, Paul means a previously hidden truth that is now revealed. In this case, the mystery refers to a plan of redemption that appears in three phases.

First, God sovereignly hardens the Jews toward Christ so that the gospel could go out to the world (see 9:14–26; 11:7–11). This hardening is "partial" in that it is temporary, lasting only until the second part of God's plan: when "the fullness of the Gentiles has come in."

What does this phrase mean? In one sense, it may refer to the full number of Gentiles whom God is calling as "a people for His name" (Acts 15:14). When all of the Gentile elect have come to faith, the Jewish hardening will be over. It may also allude to what Jesus called "the times of the Gentiles" (Luke 21:24)—a period of Gentile domination that began when Nebuchadnezzar sacked Jerusalem in 586 B.C. Ever since that time, no king from David's line has ruled in Israel. But when the fullness of Gentile supremacy is complete, the Jews will have their Davidic king.

The third part is the coming of "the Deliverer," Jesus Christ, who will establish a nation of saved Jews and reign over the entire earth in peace and righteousness during the millennial kingdom (see Isa. 11; 59:20–21).

So, once again, God turns tragedy into triumph for the Jews.

In light of all this, how should Paul's Gentile readers view the Jews: as enemies or as brothers? Paul sums up his answer in verses 28–29 of Romans 11:

> From the standpoint of the gospel they are enemies
> for your sake, but from the standpoint of God's
> choice they are beloved for the sake of the fathers;
> for the gifts and the calling of God are irrevocable.

In a way, they are enemies *and* brothers. In almost every town Paul visited, the Jews were the fiercest opponents of the gospel. Not only did they reject Christ, but they actively prevented others from hearing the message. From the perspective of those Gentiles who yearned to hear the truth, they were enemies.

Yet, from the viewpoint of election, Jews hold a unique place in God's heart. He will never recant, because of His oath to Abraham. So, while the Jews may be enemies of the gospel at times, they deserve our respect and love because of their place in God's plan of the ages.

Concluding Thoughts

As we reflect on this passage, particularly in light of the terrible suffering that Jews have endured at the hands of anti-Semites, at least four truths come to mind.

First, *the Jew is currently hardened but ultimately beloved.* Jews are generally opposed to Christ. Even so, their place in God's plan demands that we not treat them as enemies but love them as God loves them.

Second, *Gentiles are spiritually honored but undeserving.* As Gentile Christians, remembering the scrubby stock from which we were taken keeps our pride in check.

Third, *the Lord is severe with some but fair to all.* The Lord never takes His discipline beyond the point of what's fair, for Jews or Gentiles. Such a reminder encourages us to love the God who judges us and to trust Him with whatever discipline He brings.

Fourth, *Gentiles were once far off but now are grafted in.* May we as Gentile Christians never forget the grace that brought us into favor with God.

 Living Insights

From the first day Paul publicly proclaimed Christ in Damascus, the Jewish leaders determined to destroy his ministry. Perhaps they hated him because he had once been a revered Pharisee, which made his conversion all the more detestable. In their eyes, he was the worst of sinners—a traitor to his people, a double-crosser, a blasphemer. They would resort to any means necessary to stop him—even murder (see Acts 9:23; 22:22).

In light of Paul's history of ill-treatment at the hands of his own countrymen, we wouldn't fault him if he bitterly fought back. Yet, as reflected in our passage, Paul returned their anger with love and a burning desire for their salvation.

Paul's love-your-enemy ethic comes from Jesus Himself. It is the essence of "horticultural ethics," which are based on the twin virtues of gratitude and grace—gratitude for our undeserved position of favor, and grace to others in response to the grace God has poured out on us.

Is there someone in your life who is determined to pull you down? How hard has it been to return evil with good?

_____

_____

_____

How can you apply the ethics of gratitude and grace to your situation?

_____

_____

_____

God graced the Gentiles by grafting them into the covenant. He graced the Jews by designing for them a special plan of future restoration. Won't you enter into His grace today? Then share it with someone who needs it the most.

Chapter 14

UNSEARCHABLE, UNFATHOMABLE, UNMATCHED

Romans 11:30–36

May 29, 1953—the greatest day in the history of mountain climbing.

On that day, an obscure beekeeper from New Zealand and his guide set foot on virgin ground, reaching the untouched summit of the most formidable mountain in the world. The man's name was Edmund Hillary, and the peak he conquered is called Everest—a monolith that rises over 29,000 feet above sea level. That's more than five miles into the sky!

Explorers before Hillary's time considered Everest unscalable and didn't even attempt it until 1920. Before Hillary's success, ten major expeditions went up the mountain, all of which ended in failure, if not tragedy. Currently, more than four thousand men and women have tried to scale it, and of that number, 142 have died.

One can only imagine the risks and sufferings Hillary endured. Face, feet, and hands frozen rock-hard from the cold. Lungs on fire from the thin air. Life itself hanging in the balance with every precarious step on the steep precipice.

But imagine what it must have been like when Hillary finally stepped onto the summit. He had made it—he stood where no other human being ever had, on the highest point of the planet. He was on top of the world, a place as silent as light, with only the expanse of the snow-shrouded Himalayas for miles around.

As majestic as Mount Everest is, however, in comparison with the infinite heights of God's thoughts and ways, it shrinks to the infinitesimal.

In the last six verses of Romans 11, Paul stands atop a spiritual peak, looking across the vast regions of God's righteousness; His justification, sanctification, and future glorification of sinners who have turned to Him; His merciful election and sovereign predestination of a people saved from sin for a life with Himself. He cannot fully grasp the unscalable mysteries of the wisdom of God, but he can exult in them.

Let's stand with Paul on this pinnacle and extol with him the unsearchable, unfathomable, and unmatched grandeur of our God.

The Mercy of God: Unsearchable!

The attribute of God that Paul describes first is His mercy. The word *mercy* is used four times in three verses, underscoring its significance. Now, we know a lot about God's grace, His peace, and His love, but what precisely is His mercy? Dwight Pentecost called it "God's ministry to the miserable," and A. W. Tozer traces its contours this way:

> Mercy is an attribute of God, an infinite and inexhaustible energy within the divine nature which disposes God to be actively compassionate. . . .
> . . . Mercy never began to be, but from eternity was; so it will never cease to be. It will never be more since it is itself infinite; and it will never be less because the infinite cannot suffer diminution. Nothing that has occurred or will occur in heaven or earth or hell can change the tender mercies of our God. Forever His mercy stands, a boundless, overwhelming immensity of divine pity and compassion.[1]

God's mercy—His active compassion—extends to all people, whether Jews or Gentiles.

To the Gentiles

In his description of God's mercy, Paul starts with the Gentiles. He has just explained that God has introduced a new time in history, a time in which He has set aside Israel and is offering salvation to the Gentiles (Rom. 11:11–25). Wanting to highlight the mercy behind this, Paul reminds them, "You once were disobedient to God, but now have been shown mercy because of [the Jews'] disobedience" (v. 30). What exactly was the Gentiles' past? Paul describes it in one of his other letters:

> Remember that you were at that time separate from Christ, excluded from the commonwealth of Israel,

1. A. W. Tozer, *The Knowledge of the Holy* (San Francisco, Calif.: Harper and Row, Publishers, 1961), pp. 90, 91.

and strangers to the covenants of promise, having
no hope and without God in the world. (Eph. 2:12)

The Gentiles' past completely lacked God and His covenant promises. Their spiritual pedigree had no godly bloodlines, and their former master was none other than the "prince of the power of the air" (v. 2). Theirs was not a glorious past by any stretch of the imagination, and they were deserving of God's judgment.

On this pitch-dark canvas, though, God applied a single stroke of pure light. While they were still dead in their transgressions, He sent His Son, offering them life with Christ. He raised them up and seated them with His Son in the heavenly places (vv. 5–6). Only a God of unsearchable mercy would have reached so low to lift them so high.

To the Jews

In the next verse, Paul turns to the Jews. Since they had been set aside, they may have wondered if there was any hope for them. Paul answers those fears in short order:

So these [Jews] also now have been disobedient, that
because of the mercy shown to you [Gentiles] they
also may now be shown mercy. (Rom. 11:31)

Some interpreters believe that the Jews referred to in this verse—those who "may now be shown mercy"—are those who make up the believing remnant in the church age. Other Bible scholars think the verse refers to a future remnant of believing Jews—a part of national Israel whom God will turn to as His instrument for reaching the world after the Rapture of His church.

In either case, this verse reveals that the mercy God has shown to the unworthy Gentiles will be the tool He uses to redeem the equally unworthy Jews who turn in faith to Jesus, the Messiah. In other words, the Jews' disobedience opened the door of God's mercy to the Gentiles, and God's mercy to the Gentiles will open the door of His mercy to the Jews.

What a God of unsearchable mercy!

To All

Who has received unsearchable mercy from God? Jews. Gentiles. Everyone!

For God has shut up all in disobedience so that He
may show mercy to all. (v. 32)

107

The Greek term used here for "shut up," *synkleio*, is used in Luke to picture fish helplessly caught in a net (Luke 5:6). In Romans 11:32, however, the term communicates an even more graphic image, as the *Theological Dictionary of the New Testament* notes: "Paul seems quite plainly to have the figure of the prison before him. . . . Men are for Paul shut up in the prison of sin."[2]

Fish tangled in a net; inmates locked behind bars. These are the images of humankind that Paul has been building up to throughout his entire letter: "All have sinned and fall short of the glory of God" (3:23). Because of their disobedience, all people are locked in a spiritual dungeon so that "they have no possibility of escape except as God's mercy releases them."[3]

If disobedience is our prison, then mercy is our key to freedom. And what an unsearchable mercy it is! Locked in a dungeon of our own making, our sentence was death—a sentence we fully deserved. But God made sure that our disobedience didn't have the last word. He gave us *the* Word—our Savior, Jesus Christ, who took our sentence on Himself to set us free, all to display God's unsearchable mercy.

The Mind of God: Unfathomable!

Having pondered the unsearchable mercy of God, Paul now turns to explore another of God's attributes—His unfathomable mind. In the language of a doxology, he praises God's knowledge and wisdom while at the same time revealing that they are beyond human understanding.

Exclamations Needing No Proof

> Oh, the depth of the riches both of the wisdom
> and knowledge of God! How unsearchable are His
> judgments and unfathomable His ways! (Rom. 11:33)

Paul chooses words dense in theological meaning to weave a rich tapestry for us. For example, the term for "depth," *bathos*, describes things that are hidden in deep mystery—so deep that no human knowledge will ever reach it. God's knowledge and wisdom,

---

2. *Theological Dictionary of the New Testament*, ed. Gerhard Friedrich, translated and edited by Geoffrey W. Bromiley (1971; reprint, Grand Rapids, Mich.: William B. Eerdmans Publishing Co., 1993), vol. 7, p. 746.

3. C. E. B. Cranfield, *A Critical and Exegetical Commentary on the Epistle to the Romans* (Edinburgh, Scotland: T. and T. Clark, 1979), vol. 2, p. 587.

then, lie in the bottomless *bathos* of His infinite character.

Likewise, the words for "unsearchable" and "unfathomable" are thick with theological importance. Applied in a hunting context, "unsearchable" indicates an animal that is untrackable, while "unfathomable" describes one that is undetectable.[4] In other words, God's mind is so far above ours that we'd never be able to track His thoughts, and even if we could, they would be so foreign to our own understanding that we wouldn't even recognize them. Or as one scholar put it, "The mystery of God's way of judgment with Israel that leads to grace . . . cannot be given any theoretical human answer."[5]

Questions Needing No Answer

After his glorious exclamations, Paul asks three questions—questions that need no answer.

> For who has known the mind of the Lord, or who became His counselor? Or who has first given to Him that it might be paid back to Him again? (vv. 34–35)

Eugene Peterson puts these questions in today's speech:

> "Is there anyone around who can explain God?
> Anyone smart enough to tell him what to do?
> Anyone who has done him such a huge favor that
> God has to ask his advice?"[6]

Of course not. These questions, by the way, are quoted from the Old Testament: the first from Isaiah 40:13, and the second from Job 41:11. In the Job passage, God eloquently and forcefully proclaims the mysteries of His knowledge and wisdom after Job and his "counselors" have debated each other throughout the book, each presuming to understand God's ways. With an interrogation that spans four chapters, God indicts Job and the others for their

---

4. *Theological Dictionary of the New Testament*, ed. Gerhard Kittel, translated and edited by Geoffrey W. Bromiley (1964; reprint, Grand Rapids, Mich.: William B. Eerdmans Publishing Co., 1993), vol. 1, pp. 357, 358.

5. *Theological Dictionary of the New Testament*, ed. Gerhard Kittel and Gerhard Friedrich, translated and abridged in one volume by Geoffrey W. Bromiley (1985; reprint, Grand Rapids, Mich.: William B. Eerdmans Publishing Co., 1992), p. 58.

6. Eugene H. Peterson, *The Message: The New Testament in Contemporary English* (Colorado Springs, Colo.: NavPress, 1993), pp. 327–28.

arrogance. Humbled, Job offers this response:

> "I know that You can do all things,
> And that no purpose of Yours can be thwarted. . . .
> Therefore I have declared that which I did not
>   understand,
> Things too wonderful for me, which I did not
>   know." . . .
> "I have heard of You by the hearing of the ear;
> But now my eye sees You;
> Therefore I retract,
> And I repent in dust and ashes."
> (Job 42:2, 3b, 5–6)

Paul, standing on this spiritual Everest, sees what Job saw centuries before—that God's ways are unknowable, that His mind is unfathomable. And the only proper response to such a revelation is praise!

The Majesty of God: Unmatched!

Finally, Paul considers the majesty of God—a majesty that is unmatched in events both temporal and eternal.

In Temporal Events

> For from Him and through Him and to Him are all
> things. (Rom. 11:36a)

The Greek version of this phrase contains no verb. Modern translators have added "are" for clarity—and rightly so, since proper English requires it. But whatever the Greek lacks in verbs, it more than makes up for in prepositions. This phrase, in fact, contains three prepositions—all of them significant. First, "all things," meaning all things in creation, are *from* God—originate, have their source, in Him. Second, "all things" are *through* God—He channels them to us. And finally, "all things" are *to* God—He is their destiny. In other words, Paul praises "God as the Originator, the Sustainer, and the Goal of all creation."[7] His majesty in temporal events is unmatched!

---

7. Leon Morris, *The Epistle to the Romans* (1988; reprint, Grand Rapids, Mich.: William B. Eerdmans Publishing Co., 1992), p. 429.

In Eternal Glory

To Him be the glory forever. Amen. (v. 36b)

God's majesty extends beyond this world. One day, this creation will end, and God will make everything new (Rev. 21:1). His glory, though, will never end (v. 27). Commentator C. E. B. Cranfield eloquently explains the importance of this final phrase:

> So the discussion of chapters 9–11 comes to its natural and fitting conclusion in a doxology. Paul has certainly not provided neat answers to the baffling questions which arise in connexion with the subject matter of these three chapters. He has certainly not swept away all the difficulties. But, if we have followed him through these chapters with serious and open-minded attentiveness, we may well feel that he has given us enough to enable us to repeat the "Amen" of his doxology in joyful confidence that the deep mystery which surrounds us is neither a nightmare mystery of meaninglessness nor a dark mystery of arbitrary omnipotence but the mystery which will never turn out to be anything other than the mystery of the altogether good and merciful and faithful God.[8]

We might add to Cranfield's list of adjectives: unsearchable, unfathomable, and unmatched!

 Living Insights

Praising the character of God, as Paul did in Romans 11:30–36, is not an exercise meant to remain in our heads. It's meant to saturate our hearts, to be experienced and expressed by all believers, both corporately and privately. God intended us to cherish His unsearchable mercy. To marvel at His unfathomable mind. To praise His unmatched majesty.

It's often hard, though, to worship Him privately. We struggle to carve out daily time for the Lord. We're frequently too preoccupied

---

8. Cranfield, *The Epistle to the Romans*, p. 592.

with things like finances, responsibilities, and relationships to quietly focus on Him. We find ourselves having little energy left over for God. We're tired, unfocused, and stressed out. Hardly a combination conducive to the healthy worship of God.

How can we learn to become more worshipful in our private lives? Perhaps a good way to start is to cultivate the habit of meeting with God on a daily basis. Monday through Saturday, in the same place, at the same time, sit down with your Bible and a desire to experience God. Through the Scriptures and prayer, you'll encounter the Lord, and once you've met with Him, worship will begin to flow naturally.

As you contemplate how to foster worship, consider these illuminating words from Barry Leisch:

> Our worship stands or falls on our understanding of the character of God. A list of God's attributes would at least include God's wisdom, goodness, righteousness, justice, love, eternal existence, changelessness, omnipresence, omniscience, and omnipotence.[9]

Add to Leisch's list of attributes unsearchable mercy, unfathomable ways, and unmatched majesty, and you'll have a solid foundation for a healthy private worship of our Lord.

---

9. Barry Liesch, *People in the Presence of God: Models and Direction for Worship* (Grand Rapids, Mich.: Zondervan Publishing House, 1988), p. 26.

BOOKS FOR
PROBING FURTHER

Paul tackles some pretty heavy paradoxes in Romans 6–11, doesn't he? For example, we're united with Christ, but we still sin because of our relationship to Adam. We're pronounced righteous by God, yet we're not actually righteous in all that we do and think. We're indwelled by the Spirit, but we still struggle with the flesh. God is completely sovereign over all we do. Yet our choices really matter, and we're held responsible for them.

Those will keep the neurons in your noggin firing for awhile, won't they? Hopefully this study has helped you grapple with these truths and has magnified the grace and goodness of God in the process. If you want to dig deeper, the following resources will help.

Barton, Bruce B., David R. Veerman, and Neil Wilson. *Romans.* Life Application Bible Commentary Series. Wheaton, Ill.: Tyndale House Publishers, 1992.

Boice, James Montgomery. *Romans, Volume 2: The Reign of Grace (Romans 5:1–8:39).* Grand Rapids, Mich.: Baker Book House, 1992.

————. *Romans, Volume 3: God and History (Romans 9–11).* Grand Rapids, Mich.: Baker Book House, 1993.

Bridges, Jerry. *Transforming Grace: Living Confidently in God's Unfailing Love.* Colorado Springs, Colo.: NavPress, 1991.

Carson, D. A. *Divine Sovereignty and Human Responsibility: Biblical Perspectives in Tension.* Grand Rapids, Mich.: Baker Book House, 1994.

Dieter, Melvin E., Anthony A. Hoekema, Stanley M. Horton, J. Robertson McQuilkin, and John F. Walvoord. *Five Views on Sanctification.* Grand Rapids, Mich.: Academie Books, Zondervan Publishing House, 1987.

Feinberg, John S., Norman Geisler, Bruce Reichenbach, and Clark Pinnock. *Predestination and Free Will: Four Views of Divine Sovereignty and Human Freedom.* Downers Grove, Ill.: InterVarsity

Press, 1986. Though we no longer consider Clark Pinnock's views to be representative of orthodox Evangelical beliefs, the format of this book allows each author to present his view and then be challenged by the other authors, providing enlightening discussion.

Harrison, Everett F. "Romans." In *The Expositor's Bible Commentary.* Vol. 10. Gen. ed. Frank E. Gaebelein. Grand Rapids, Mich.: Regency Reference Library, Zondervan Publishing House, 1976.

Lightner, Robert P. *Sin, the Savior, and Salvation.* Nashville, Tenn.: Thomas Nelson Publishers, 1991.

Manning, Brennan. *Abba's Child: The Cry of the Heart for Intimate Belonging.* Colorado Springs, Colo.: NavPress, 1994.

Morris, Leon. *The Epistle to the Romans.* 1988. Reprint, Grand Rapids, Mich.: William B. Eerdmans Publishing Co., 1992.

Packer, J. I. *Evangelism and the Sovereignty of God.* Downers Grove, Ill.: InterVarsity Press, 1961.

————. *Keep in Step with the Spirit.* Old Tappan, N.J.: Fleming H. Revell Co., 1984.

Smedes, Lewis. *Union with Christ: A Biblical View of the New Life in Jesus Christ.* 2d ed., revised. Grand Rapids, Mich.: William B. Eerdmans Publishing Co., 1983.

Sproul, R. C. *The Invisible Hand: Do All Things Really Work for Good?* Dallas, Tex.: Word Publishing, 1996.

Stott, John. *Romans: God's Good News for the World.* Downers Grove, Ill.: InterVarsity Press, 1994.

Swindoll, Charles R. *The Grace Awakening.* Dallas, Tex.: Word Publishing, 1990.

————. *Growing Deep in the Christian Life.* Portland, Ore.: Multnomah Press, 1986.

Walvoord, John F., and Roy B. Zuck, eds. *The Bible Knowledge Commentary.* New Testament edition. Colorado Springs, Colo.: Chariot Victor Publishing, 1983.

Yancey, Philip. *What's So Amazing about Grace?* Grand Rapids, Mich.: Zondervan Publishing House, 1997.

Some of these books may be out of print and available only through a library. For those currently available, please contact your local Christian bookstore. Books by Charles R. Swindoll may be obtained through Insight for Living, as well as some books by other authors.

Insight for Living also offers study guides on many books of the Bible, as well as on a variety of issues and Bible characters. For more information, see the ordering instructions that follow and contact the office that serves you.